Intro to Science

Teacher Guide

Intro to Science Teacher Guide

Third Edition, 2024
Copyright @ Elemental Science, Inc.

ISBN # 978-1-953490-23-0

Printed in the USA for worldwide distribution

For more copies write to:
Elemental Science
PO Box 79
Niceville, FL 32588
support@elementalscience.com

Copyright Policy

Classical SCIENCE Quick Start Guide

In a Nutshell

Students will get a basic introduction to science by:

- ✓ Listening to **scientific information** from weekly introductions and extra books.

- ✓ Playing with **hands-on science** through demonstrations and hands-on projects.

- ✓ Dictating what they have learned and seen using simple **notebooking**.

See p. 8 for a list of the topics explored in this program.

What You Need

In addition to this guide, you will need the following:

1. **The student materials** - You can purchase either the *Intro to Science Student Pages* or the *Intro to Science Lapbooking Templates*. (Get a glimpse of these options on p. 14.)

2. **The demonstration supplies** - See a full list starting on p. 15 or save yourself the time and purchase the *Intro to Science Experiment Kit*.

You can also purchase the *The Usborne Children's Encyclopedia* for the encyclopedia pages and/or the *The Handbook of Nature Study* by Anne Botsford Comstock for the nature study option. Get links to these books here:

🖱 https://elementalscience.com/blogs/resources/intro

How It Works

None of the assignments in this guide are marked "optional" because they are all optional! This is the first year of science for a student, so look at this guide as a buffet of options for each week. A week could look like the following:

- ✍ **Read** the scripted introduction with your students. If they would like to learn more, you can read the encyclopedia pages or one of the library books.

- ✍ **Do** the weekly demonstration or the nature study with the students. If they would like to do more, you can choose from the coordinating activities.

- ✍ **Write** down what the students have learned and seen in a way that is appropriate for their skills.

For a more detailed explanation of the components in each lesson, we highly recommend checking out the peek inside this program on pp. 6-7 and reading the introduction starting on p. 9. Otherwise, the first lesson begins on p. 24.

Table of Contents

A Peek Inside the Teacher Guide

The teacher guide is your buffet of options for creating memorable science lessons!

1. & 2. Two Scheduling Options

See what you could do and when with the two grid-style scheduling options. There are a 2-day-a-week (1) and a 5-day-a-week (2) schedules. These schedules break down the buffet of options into manageable chunks so that you can proceed with confidence.

Read

3. Weekly Topic

Focus on a main idea for each week. This will be explored through the introduction, hands-on projects, and activities.

4. Scripted Introduction

Know how to share the weekly topic with your students in a meaningful way. These scripted talks and suggested demonstrations will help you introduce what your students need to know.

5. Read-Alouds

Gather more information with suggested pages in a popular children's encyclopedias and a list of library books you can look for.

Do

6. Scientific Demonstrations

Show science with a weekly hands-on science activity that coordinates with the topic. This section includes the supplies you will need, along with scripted introductions.

The easy-to-follow steps and scripted explanations make it a snap to complete the scientific demonstration.

7. Nature Study

Find science in nature with these related nature study ideas. Each of these activities will help you prepare and execute an outdoor nature study that relates to the weekly topic.

8. Coordinating Activities

Get ideas for additional art projects, snacks, games, and science activities that relate to the week's topic.

Write

9. Student Diary Assignments

Record what your students have learned with the student diary. The directions for these pages are included for your convenience in the guide.

10. Lapbook Assignments

Create a scrapbook of what your students have learned with the lapbooking templates. (Note—*We typically recommend choosing this option or the student diary option, not both at the same time.*)

Sample page 22

22

✓ Muffin tin

Steps to Complete

1. Read the following introduction to your students:

   Remember earlier we saw how solids melt into ⬤6 w, we are going to turn our solid wax crayon into liquid wax by he___ up. Then, we are going to let our crayon muffins cool to see what happens!

2. Place the foil muffin cup liners into a muffin tin. Let the students break the crayons into pieces and place them in the cups.

3. [Parents Only] Preheat the oven to 300°F. Once the students have finished place the muffin tin in the oven for about 15 minutes, just enough time for the crayons to melt. Then, using a hot mitt, remove the tin and let the students observe, asking them:

   ? What happened to the crayons in our muffin-cup?

4. Let the tray cool for about 30 minutes. Then, come back and observe the crayon muffins again, asking the students:

   ? Have the crayon muffins changed?

Explanation

Then, read the following explanation to them:

   We saw our crayons melt into a liquid crayon muffin with the heat from the oven. Then, as they cooled off, the liquid turned into a solid crayon muffin!

   (*Note*—Keep your crayon muffins for use later in the week.)

Nature Study: Finding Wax Coatings

This year, your nature study time will mainly focus on developing the students' awareness of the world around them. For your own personal knowledge about guiding nature study, I recommend that you read pp. 1-23 in the Handbook of Nature Study.

Preparation

⚬ Waxy coating ___ nd in nature on most pine trees, so that is the focus of your nature study this we⬤7 670-674 in the *Handbook of Nature Study* to learn more about pine trees.

Outdoor Time

⚬ Go on a walk with the students to see if you can find any pine trees to observe. Allow the students to observe the tree and ask any questions they may have. You can use the information you have learned from reading the *Handbook of Nature Study* to answer their

Intro to Science Unit 1 Intro to Chemistry ~ Week 1 Solids and Liquids

---

Sample page 23

23

questions or to share information about what they are observing.

Coordinating Activities

These following activities will help you ___ reinforce the week's topic and main idea.

✂ Art – (Coloring with Cookies) ___ ⬤8 ents their crayon cookies they made during their experiment. Let them col___ of their choice using their crayon cookies.

✂ Snack – (Solid Popsicles) Point out to the students that popsicles are solid, ask what happens when they take a bit of their popsicle and let it sit in their mouth for minute.

✂ Game – (Will it melt?) Let the students choose several foods that they want to see melt (such as chocolate or crackers). Place them in a muffin tin and heat them in the oven for five minutes, watching carefully. Observe what happens.

Write – Simple Notebooking

Student Diary

☐ Main Idea Page – Have the students color the coloring page fou___

☐ Demonstration Sheet – After you do the demonstration, fill o⬤9 tration sheet found on SD p. _ with the students.

☐ Nature Journal Sheet – After you have your nature study time, fill out the nature journal sheet found on SD p. _ with the students. The students can sketch what they have seen or you can write down their observations.

☐ Art Page – Have the students use SD p. _ to complete the art activity.

Lapbooking Templates

☐ Weekly Mini-book – Have the students cut out and color the Solids and Liquids Mini-book on LT p. 7. You can have them cut out the main idea graphic included and glue it in the interior of the ___ ⬤10 ___ you can write a sentence with what they have learned from the week for the___ of the mini book. Once the students are done, have them glue the booklet in___ apbook.

☐ Overall Lapbook – Have the students cut out the "My Chemistry Projects" pocket on LT p. 13. Have them glue the pocket into the lapbook and add the coloring project they just did to the pocket.

Intro to Science Unit 1 Intro to Chemistry ~ Week 1 Solids and Liquids

---

List of Topics Covered in This Program

Chemistry Unit

- ✓ Solids
- ✓ Liquids
- ✓ Mixtures
- ✓ Dilution
- ✓ Density
- ✓ Crystals
- ✓ Colors
- ✓ Freezing

Physics Unit

- ✓ Forces
- ✓ Gravity
- ✓ Magnets
- ✓ Inclined Planes
- ✓ Sound
- ✓ Light

Geology Unit

- ✓ Fossils
- ✓ Rocks
- ✓ Metamorphic Rock
- ✓ Volcanoes (Igneous Rock)
- ✓ Sedimentary Rock
- ✓ Compass

Meteorology Unit

- ✓ Sun
- ✓ Water Cycle
- ✓ Seasons
- ✓ Wind
- ✓ Tornadoes
- ✓ Thermometer

Botany Unit

- ✓ Plants
- ✓ Flowers
- ✓ Seeds
- ✓ Leaves
- ✓ Stems
- ✓ Roots

Zoology Unit

- ✓ Mammals
- ✓ Reptiles
- ✓ Birds
- ✓ Butterflies
- ✓ Insects
- ✓ Fish

Quick Links

The following page contains quick access to the activity links suggested in this guide along with several helpful downloads:

🖱 https://elementalscience.com/blogs/resources/intro

Introduction to the 3rd Edition

It has been more than 13 years since the first edition of *Intro to Science* was released. With each edition, the format has been refined, but the method has always been based on the same three keys to teaching science:

1. Read about science.
2. Do, or rather play with, science.
3. Write about science.

If you want to learn more about these keys, check out this free conference session:

⤷ *The 3 Keys to Teaching Science* - https://elementalscience.com/blogs/news/3-keys

In this guide are the tools you need to teach science using the Classic Method found in *Success in Science: A Manual for Excellence in Science Education*. This method is loosely based on the ideas for classical science education that are laid out in *The Well-Trained Mind: A Guide to Classical Education at Home* by Jessie Wise and Susan Wise Bauer.

In *Success in Science: A Manual for Excellence in Science Education*, we write that the goal for preschool science is simply to introduce your students to the world around them. It is with this goal in mind that we have written *Intro to Science*. This year, your students will explore the wonderful world of science through a buffet of weekly topics, hands-on projects, books, and activities. All this will work together to build a basic framework, or bucket, the students can fill with information during the elementary years. If you would like to learn more about our philosophy for preschool science, check out this article:

⤷ *Should you bother with preschool science?* https://elementalscience.com/blogs/news/should-you-bother-with-preschool-science-in-your-homeschool

Let's take a closer took at what you will find in this guide.

A Quick Note

Nothing in this guide is marked optional. This is done on purpose because everything in this guide is optional! Our idea is that this is the first year of science for a student. It's meant to be an introduction to peak a student's interest in science. So look at this guide as a buffet of options for each week, not as a list of things that you have to complete.

Unit Overview Sheets

Each unit will begin with an overview sheet that shows the list of topics, the supplies you will need, and the books that are scheduled by week. These are meant to give you a snapshot of the unit. Please feel free to swap the units around, but do keep the weeks within the unit in order as you work through this program.

Schedule Options

We have included scheduling options, but these are mere suggestions, not hard-and-fast rules. Remember that *Intro to Science* is a buffet-style introduction, so pick and choose what works for you and your students. We would suggest scheduling science for two (20-minute) blocks a week or five (10-minute) blocks a week. There are two potential schedules for you to give an idea of how you could schedule each week—one that breaks the assignments over two days, and one that breaks these assignments over five days. Each of these schedules has three sections to reflect the three keys to teaching science—read, do, and write (more about these in a moment). You can choose to use these as your guide or create your own schedule using one of the blank scheduling templates in the appendix on pp. 202-203 of this guide.

Read – Information Gathering

The Weekly Topic

The main purpose of having a weekly topic is to create a focus for your studies for the week. Each week, this section will provide the main idea.

Scripted Introduction

After the weekly topic, you will find a scripted introduction. This introduction may contain simple explanations, brief demonstrations, and/or guided observations for you to use when introducing the students to the week's topic. We have provided a preplanned script for you to read, but feel free to use your own words or edit the script as you communicate the information. The main purpose of introducing the topic is to share with your students what they will be studying for the week. Your introduction should only take five to fifteen minutes because of the students' short attention spans.

After you introduce the week's topic (or during, if you have a fidgety student), you can have the students color the coordinating coloring page for their scrapbook.

Read-Alouds

During the preschool years, students usually love to be read to, and science is a good topic to explore through books at this age. For this reason, we have included options for you to read aloud to your students. The first is encyclopedia pages, which all come from the following resource:

    📖 *The Usborne Children's Encyclopedia* (2014 edition)

The second is a list of library books for you to choose from each week. These books are suggestions that you can get from your local library. We have not previewed each and every book, so be sure to do so before you read them to the students.

Do – Hands-on Projects

Scientific Demonstrations

Scientific demonstrations are designed to help the students see the science of their environment in action, whereas nature studies are designed to aid the students in learning about the world around them through discovery and observation. (Note—*If you want to read more about the differences between demonstrations and experiments, check out the following article: https://elementalscience.com/blogs/news/89905795-scientific-demonstrations-or-experiments*)

These generally use easy-to-find materials and tie into what is being studied. You will find several sections for the scientific demonstration:

❑ The Materials Needed
❑ The Steps to Complete (*including a scripted introduction and detailed instructions*)
❑ The Explanation (*including the expected results and a scripted explanation*)
  All scripted text, introductions, and explanations will be in this font.

These demonstrations are designed to provide a beginner's look at the scientific method and how scientific tests work. Even so, it is not necessary to ask the students to predict the outcome of the demonstration because they have no knowledge base to determine what the answer should be. However, if your students enjoy predicting, or they are able to tell you what will happen, please feel free to let them do so. After you finish the demonstration, you can have the students fill out a demonstration sheet.

Nature Study

The nature studies included in the hands-on project sections also coordinate with the weekly topic. If you choose to do these, you will need the following:

📖 *The Handbook of Nature Study* by Anne Botsford Comstock (1986 edition) (Note—*This book is more of a teacher reference than a book to read to your students. The idea is that you as the teacher will read the material ahead of time so that you will have the knowledge to assist your students as they learn through their own observations of nature. It is NOT designed to be read to the student.*)

The purpose of these nature studies is to have the students learn about the world around them through discovery and observation. (**Note**—*If you want to read more about the differences between demonstrations and experiments, check out the following article: https://elementalscience.com/blogs/news/nature-study*)

You will find two sections for the nature study:

❑ Preparation
❑ Outdoore Time

After you finish the nature study activity, you can have the students fill out a nature journal sheet for their scrapbook. Allow them to draw what they would like, or glue a picture on the page instead. At this stage, it is best for you to write down their observations for them.

Coordinating Activities

Coordinating activities are meant to reinforce what the students are learning. In this guide, we have included additional art projects, snacks, games, and science activities that will tie into the weekly topic.

Write – Simple Notebooking

We have two options for your students to record what they have learned, both of which are seperate purchases. You can peek inside both of them on p. 14.

The Student Diary

The *Intro to Science Student Diary* is made up of simple journal sheets where the students record what they have learned and done over the year. They include coloring pages, demonstration sheets, activity pages, and nature journal sheets to use each week. The following is a description of how the individual scrapbook pages are designed to be used:

- **Main Idea Page** – Read the main idea at the bottom of the page to the students as you have them color the picture.
- **Demonstration Sheet** – Have the students tell you what they learned from the scientific demonstration, and write it down for them on the lines provided. Include any applicable pictures in the boxes provided.
- **Nature Journal Sheet** – Have the students tell you what they learned from the nature study activity, and write it down for them on the lines provided. Include any applicable pictures in the boxes provided.
- **Art Page** – Have your students draw a picture or paste in a picture of the craft project they made on the sheet provided.

The Lapbooking Templates

The *Intro to Science Lapbooking Templates* includes a set of templates for six lapbooks to go along with this program. Each lapbook has six mini-books (one for each weekly topic) a project folder template, and a color cover for the lapbook. We have included a pre-written main idea sentence to paste into each mini-book, or you can have the students copy the main idea sentence into the mini-book.

Additional Resources

The following webpage contains quick links to the activities suggested in this guide, along with several helpful downloads:

🖱 https://elementalscience.com/blogs/resources/intro

Final Thoughts

As the author and publisher of this curriculum, I encourage you to contact us with any questions or problems that you might have concerning *Intro to Science* at support@ elementalscience.com. We will be more than happy to answer them as soon as we are able. I hope that you enjoy this third edition of *Intro to Science*!

~ Paige Hudson

Student Options At-a-Glance

Pick one of these options so that your students can document their introduction to science!

The Student Diary

The *Intro to Science Student Diary* contains main idea pages (1), demonstration sheets (2), nature journal sheets (3), and art pages (4). These pages allow your students to create a scrapbook-style workbook, or lab manual, with what they learned in this program.

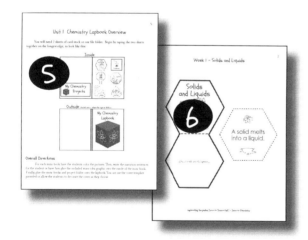

The Lapbooking Templates

The *Intro to Science Lapbooking Templates* contain lapbooking over sheets (5) and a set of mini-books with preprinted narrations (6) for the students to use. The mini-books are designed to be cut out and glued into the students' lapbooks (or file folders) for a total of six lapbooks for the year. Alternatively, you can use these mini-books to create a single large lapbook.

See both of these options at:

https://elementalscience.com/collections/intro-to-science

Materials Listed By Unit

Chemistry Unit

Week	Introduction Props	Hands-on Project Materials	Coordinating Activities Supplies
1	Ice, Crayon	Crayons, Foil muffin-cup liners, Muffin tin	Paper, Popsicles, Chocolate or Crackers
2	Plate, Paintbrush, Cup	Juice, Measuring cups, 4 Cups, Dirt, Water	Pudding mix, Milk Several cups, Kool-Aid mix, Paint (one color and white), Paintbrush, Dirt
3	Glass jar, Water, Spoon, Oil	Glass jar, Water, Objects to test, Bucket of water	Chalk, Water, Paper, 9 by 13 Pan, Several types of fruit, Glass jar, Oil, Water, Food coloring
4	Pictures of various types of crystals (or several rocks with crystals)	Plastic bowl (or disposable pie pan), Sponge (cut into 1-inch cubes), Water, Salt, Liquid bluing, Ammonia, Measuring spoons	2 Bowls, Sugar, Salt, Paper, Epsom salts, warm water, a glass, food coloring (blue is best), a paintbrush
5	3 Glasses, Food coloring (blue and yellow)	4 Clear glasses, Eyedropper, Food coloring (red, yellow, blue), Water, Prism	Sugar cookies, Icing in different colors, Shallow dish, Milk, Food coloring (red, yellow, and blue), Liquid dish soap, Paint (red, yellow, and blue), Paper
6	Ice, Plate	Ice cube tray (or small plastic containers), Various household liquids	Various frozen foods, Food coloring, Water, Paper

Physics Unit

Week	Introduction Props	Hands-on Project Materials	Coordinating Activities Supplies
1	Marble	Toy car, String (2 feet long), Tape	Paint, Paintbrush, Cutting board, Different kinds of round fruits and vegetables, Several rubber bands, Measuring tape

Week	Introduction Props	Hands-on Project Materials	Coordinating Activities Supplies
2	Pencil	Several objects of varying size and weight (crayon, pompom, paper, balloon, paper clip, and more)	Apple, Balloons, Paper, Eyedropper, Paint
3	Bar magnet, Several metal paper clips	String, Magnet, Variety of metal and nonmetal objects	Sugar cookie, Red and blue M&M's, Paper, Thin cardboard, Paint, Several magnetic objects, Magnet
4	Long wooden block, Toy car	Marble, Bouncy ball, Thin wooden board or thick cardboard, Blocks, Tape (or other marker)	Graham crackers, Marshmallows, Bowl of water, Eye dropper, Wax paper, Marbles, Plate, Paint, Block, Paper, Thin cardboard
5	*No supplies needed.*	An empty yogurt container, Wax paper, Rubber band, Salt, Sound makers	2 Paper plates, Paint, Tape, Beans, Rice Krispies cereal, Bowl, Milk, Toilet paper tube
6	*No supplies needed.*	Bubble solution and wand, Plate	Flashlights, Reflective materials, Paper, Glue

Geology Unit

Week	Introduction Props	Hands-on Project Materials	Coordinating Activities Supplies
1	Several pictures of fossils (or an actual fossil)	Air dry clay, Rubber insects or shells, Rolling pin	Sugar cookie dough, Several plant or animal stamps or stencils, Gray or brown paint, Paper
2	Several rocks from your area	Rock, Hammer	Rock candy, Several rocks you have collected, Several colors of paint, Medium sized rock
3	Several metamorphic rocks	Six different colors of crayon, Old grater, Aluminum foil, Bowl, Hot water	Peanut butter (or other nut butter), jelly, bread, Crayons, Paper, Cardboard, Hair dryer, Several rocks
4	*No supplies needed.*	Scissors or a knife, Tube of a toothpaste, Empty plastic yogurt container, Dirt	Paint (black, gray, orange, red), Paper, Paper cup, Crackers (saltines or Ritz™), Can of CheeseWhiz™

Week	Introduction Props	Hands-on Project Materials	Coordinating Activities Supplies
5	Sandstone	Glass or plastic jar with a lid, Sand, Gravel, Pebbles or small rocks, Water	Graham crackers Peanut butter, Sugar, Mini chocolate chips, Sand, Glue, Pebbles, Bread loaf pan, Plastic wrap, Paint, Sand, Paper
6	Compass, Map	Compass, Small treasure or candy, Paper, Pen	Sugar cookies, Icing, Pencil, Paper, Pin, Milk jug, Knife, Magnet

Meteorology Unit

Week	Introduction Props	Hands-on Project Materials	Coordinating Activities Supplies
1	*No supplies needed.*	Muffin tin, Foil, Clear plastic wrap, Marshmallows, Chocolate chips, Butter	Orange, SunPrint paper, Several squares of red, yellow, and orange tissue paper, Paper
2	Water Cycle Picture from pg. 188 of the Appendix	Clear glass jar, Jar lid or bowl, Ice cubes, Hot water	Egg whites, Cream of Tartar, Vanilla, Sugar, Small spray bottle or eyedropper, Blue paint, Paper
3	*No supplies needed.*	Weather Stickers (appendix p. 194)	Bananas, Grapes, Strawberries, Raisins, Carrots, Skewers, Paper, Seasonal pictures from magazines
4	*No supplies needed.*	Bubble mixture, Bubble wand	Blue Jell-O, Cool Whip, Container of bubbles, Paper, String, 2 Sticks
5	Pictures of tornadoes	Pint-sized Mason jar, Dish soap, Vinegar, Water, Glitter	Frozen fruit, Ice cream, Milk or juice, Thick paintbrush, Paper, Black and white paint, Plate, 2 Plastic bottles, Washer, Duct tape
6	Thermometer	2 Clear cups, Food coloring, Water (hot and ice-cold), Thermometer	Variety of hot and cold foods, Pictures of things to do or wear when it is hot or cold, Modeling clay, Food coloring, Water, Clear straw, Rubbing alcohol, Small bottle

Botany Unit

Week	Introduction Props	Hands-on Project Materials	Coordinating Activities Supplies
1	Small potted plant	Small pot, Bean seed, Potting soil, Water	Potato or carrot sticks, Celery, Lettuce, Berries, Tissue paper squares (brown, green, red, and purple), Glue, Paper
2	Plant with a flower	Tulip, Razor or knife, Magnifying glass, Q-tip	Cake with icing flowers, A large White T-shirt (100% cotton), Cardboard, Flowers and Leaves, Masking Tape, Newspaper or Towels, Hammer, Paint, Paper
3	Lima bean seed (soaked overnight)	3 Bean seeds, Paper towel, Plastic baggie, Tape, and Water	Different fruits and seeds to eat, Red paint, Apple, Plate, Paper, Paintbrush, Glue, Seeds
4	Bean plant	Bean plant, Paper, Paper clip	Edible leaves (lettuce, spinach, kale or bok choy), Ranch dressing, Sheet of cardboard, Leaves, Crayons, Paper, Leaves, Tape, Newspaper, Hammer
5	Celery, Magnifying glass	Celery (with leaves), Food coloring, Glass, Water	Celery Sticks, Cream Cheese, Brown and green paint, Straw, Water, Paper
6	Green onion with roots	Green onion, Cup, Water	Green onion with roots, Carrot sticks or shoestring potato sticks, Green onion with roots, Paint, Paper

Zoology Unit

Week	Introduction Props	Hands-on Project Materials	Coordinating Activities Supplies
1	Pictures of mammals	Three pictures of mammals	Animal crackers, Mammal pictures from old magazines or animal stickers

Week	Introduction Props	Hands-on Project Materials	Coordinating Activities Supplies
2	Pictures of reptiles	Thermometer	Peanut butter, Powdered milk, Honey, Cocoa, Vanilla, Chopped Nuts, Raisins, Mini M&M's, Pictures of reptiles, 2 Colors of paint, Paper, Black Marker
3	Pictures of birds	Cheerios, Pipe cleaner	Mangoes, blueberries, or strawberries, Sunflower seeds, Pipe cleaners, Feathers, Paint, Paper
4	Pictures of butterflies	Butterfly life cycle cards from appendix	Lettuce, Eyedropper, Paint, Paper, Glitter, Sequins, Glue, Butterfly outline on paper
5	Pictures of invertebrates	Plate, Several types of food (i.e., bread, cheese, crackers, honey, and fruit)	Gummy worms, 1 Large and 1 small Styrofoam balls, Black paint, Googly eyes, Black pipe cleaners, Paint, Thick string, Paper
6	Pictures of fish	*No supplies needed.*	Goldfish crackers, Paper, Watercolor paints, Glitter, Construction paper, Paper clips, Magnet, Dowel rod, String

Intro to Science

Unit 1: Intro to Chemistry

Intro to Chemistry Unit Overview

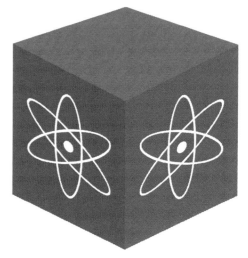

Sequence for Study

- ✦ Week 1: Solids and liquids
- ✦ Week 2: Mixtures
- ✦ Week 3: Density
- ✦ Week 4: Crystals
- ✦ Week 5: Colors
- ✦ Week 6: Freezing

Supplies Needed for the Unit

Week	Introduction Props	Hands-on Project Materials	Coordinating Activities Supplies
1	Ice, Crayon	Crayons, Foil muffin-cup liners, Muffin tin	Paper, Popsicles, Chocolate or Crackers
2	Plate, Paintbrush, Cup	Juice, Measuring cups, 4 Cups, Dirt, Water	Pudding mix, Milk Several cups, Kool-Aid mix, Paint (one color and white), Paintbrush, Dirt
3	Glass jar, Water, Spoon, Oil	Glass jar, Water, Objects to test, Bucket of water	Chalk, Water, Paper, 9 by 13 Pan, Several types of fruit, Glass jar, Oil, Water, Food coloring
4	Pictures of various types of crystals (or several rocks with crystals)	Plastic bowl (or disposable pie pan), Sponge (cut into 1-inch cubes), Water, Salt, Liquid bluing, Ammonia, Measuring spoons	2 Bowls, Sugar, Salt, Paper, Epsom salts, warm water, a glass, food coloring (blue is best), a paintbrush
5	3 Glasses, Food coloring (blue and yellow)	4 Clear glasses, Eyedropper, Food coloring (red, yellow, blue), Water, Prism	Sugar cookies, Icing in different colors, Shallow dish, Milk, Food coloring (red, yellow, and blue), Liquid dish soap, Paint (red, yellow, and blue), Paper
6	Ice, Plate	Ice cube tray (or small plastic containers), Various household liquids	Various frozen foods, Food coloring, Water, Paper

Books Scheduled

Hands-on Projects

⌨ *Handbook of Nature Study (If you are using the nature study option.)*

Scheduled Encylopedias

⌨ *The Usborne Children's Encyclopedia*

Library Books to Look For

Week 1

⌨ *What is the world made of? All about solids, liquids and gases (Let's Read and Find out About Science) by Kathleen Weidner Zoehfeld and Paul Meisel*

⌨ *Change It!: Solids, Liquids, Gases and You (Primary Physical Science) by Adrienne Mason and Claudia Davila*

⌨ *Solids, Liquids and Gases (Starting with Science) by Ray Boudreau*

Week 2

⌨ *Liquids (States of Matter) by Carol Ryback and Jim Mezzanotte*

⌨ *Lulu's Lemonade (Math Matters) by Barbara Derubertis and Paige Billin-Frye*

Week 3

⌨ *What Is Density? (Rookie Read-About Science) by Joanne Barkan*

⌨ *Will It Float or Sink? (Rookie Read-About Science) by Melissa Stewart*

Week 4

⌨ *Crystals (The Golden Science Close-up Series)* by Robert A. Bell

⌨ *Rock and Minerals (Eye Wonder)* by DK Publishing

Week 5

⌨ *All the Colors of the Rainbow (Rookie Read-About Science) by Allan Fowler*

⌨ *The Magic School Bus Makes A Rainbow: A Book About Color by Joanna Cole*

⌨ *I Love Colors! (Hello Reader!, Level 1) by Hans Wilhelm*

Week 6

⌨ *Freezing and Melting (First Step Nonfiction) by Robin Nelson*

⌨ *Solids, Liquids, And Gases (Rookie Read-About Science) by Ginger Garrett*

Week 1: Solids and Liquids

You do not need to complete all of this in a week. Instead, choose from the following options.

2-Days-a-Week Schedule		
	Day 1	**Day 2**
Read	❑ Read the introduction with the students ❑ Read the selected pages in *The Usborne Children's Encyclopedia*	❑ Choose one or more of the additional books to read from this week
Do	❑ Complete the Scientific Demonstration "Crayon Muffins" ❑ Eat "Solid Popsicles" for snack	❑ Complete the Nature Study "Finding Waxy Coatings" ❑ Do the "Coloring with Cookies" activity
Write	❑ Color the main idea page ❑ Fill out the demonstration sheet	❑ Fill out the nature journal sheet ❑ Complete the art page

5-Days-a-Week Schedule					
	Day 1	**Day 2**	**Day 3**	**Day 4**	**Day 5**
Read	❑ Read the introduction with the students	❑ Read the selected pages in *The Usborne Children's Encyclopedia*	❑ Choose one or more of the additional books to read from this week	❑ Choose one or more of the additional books to read from this week	
Do	❑ Eat "Solid Popsicles" for snack	❑ Complete the Scientific Demonstration "Crayon Muffins"	❑ Work on the activity "Will it melt?"	❑ Do the "Coloring with Cookies" activity	❑ Complete the Nature Study "Finding Waxy Coatings"
Write	❑ Color the main idea page	❑ Fill out the demonstration sheet	❑ Complete the Solid and Liquids Mini-book	❑ Complete the art page	❑ Fill out the nature journal sheet

Read – Information Gathering

Weekly Topic

- A solid melts into a liquid.

Scripted Introduction

Have a piece of ice and a crayon on a plate in front of each student. Say to the students:

> This week, we are going to look closer at solids and liquids. The ice and the crayon in front of us are both solids. Ice is solid water, but the crayon is made from solid wax. When ice gets warm, it melts and turns into liquid water. See how that's happening right in front of us? This process is called melting.

Let them play with the ice and see firsthand how it is turning into a liquid. Then, ask the students:

> **?** Is the crayon in front of us melting?

Then, say:

> That's right! The crayon remains a solid. This is because it needs a lot more heat before it will melt and become a liquid.

Read–Alouds

Encyclopedia Pages

- *The Usborne Children's Encyclopedia* pp. 188-189 "Solids, liquids, and gases"

Library Books to Look For

- *What is the world made of? All about solids, liquids and gases (Let's Read and Find out About Science)* by Kathleen Weidner Zoehfeld and Paul Meisel
- *Change It!: Solids, Liquids, Gases and You (Primary Physical Science)* by Adrienne Mason and Claudia Davila
- *Solids, Liquids and Gases (Starting with Science)* by Ray Boudreau

Do – Hands-on Projects

Scientific Demonstration: Crayon Muffins

Materials Needed

- ✓ Crayons
- ✓ Foil muffin-cup liners

✓ Muffin tin

Steps to Complete

1. Read the following introduction to your students:

   Remember earlier we saw how solids melt into liquids? Now, we are going to turn our solid wax crayons into liquid wax by heating them up. Then, we are going to let our crayon muffins cool to see what happens!

2. Place the foil muffin cup liners into a muffin tin. Let the students break the crayons into pieces and place them in the cups.

3. {**Adults Only**} Preheat the oven to 300°F. Once the students have finished, place the muffin tin in the oven for about 15 minutes, enough time for the crayons to melt. Then, using a hot mitt, remove the tin and let the students observe, asking them:

   ? What happened to the crayons in our muffin cup?

4. Let the tray cool for about 30 minutes. Then, come back and observe the crayon muffins again, asking the students:

   ? Have the crayon muffins changed?

Explanation

Read the following explaination to the students:

We saw our crayons melt into a liquid crayon muffin with the heat from the oven. Then, as they cooled off, the liquid turned into a solid crayon muffin!

(Note—Keep your crayon muffins to use with the art activity.)

Nature Study: Finding Wax Coatings

This year, your nature study time will mainly focus on developing the students' awareness of the world around them. For your own personal knowledge about guiding this nature study, I recommend that you read pp. 1-23 in the *Handbook of Nature Study*.

Preparation

↻ Waxy coatings can be found in nature on most pine trees, so that is the focus of your nature study this week. Read pp. 670-674 in the *Handbook of Nature Study* to learn more about pine trees.

Outdoor Time

☼ Go on a walk with the students to see if you can find any pine trees to observe. Allow the students to observe the tree and ask any questions they may have. You can use the information you have learned from reading the *Handbook of Nature Study* to answer their questions or to share information about what they are observing.

Coordinating Activities

✂ **Art** – (Coloring with Cookies) Give the students their crayon cookies they made during their experiment. Let them color a picture of their choice using their crayon cookies.

✂ **Snack** – (Solid Popsicles) Point out to the students that popsicles are solid. Ask what happens when they take a bite of their popsicle and let it sit in their mouth for a minute.

✂ **Activity** – (Will it melt?) Let the students choose several foods that they want to see melt (such as chocolate or crackers). Place them in a muffin tin, and heat them in the oven for five minutes, watching carefully. Observe what happens.

Write – Simple Notebooking

Student Diary

☐ **Main Idea Page** – Have the students color the coloring page found in the *Intro to Science Student Diary* (SD) p. 9.

☐ **Demonstration Sheet** – After you do the demonstration, fill out the demonstration sheet found on SD p. 10 with the students.

☐ **Nature Journal Sheet** – After you have your nature study time, fill out the nature journal sheet found on SD p. 11 with the students. The students can sketch what they have seen, or you can write down their observations.

☐ **Art Page** – Have the students use SD p. 12 to complete the art activity.

Lapbooking Templates

📁 **Weekly Mini-book** – Have the students cut out and color the Solids and Liquids Mini-book in the *Intro to Science Lapbooking Templates* (LT) p. 9. You can have them cut out the main idea graphic included and glue it in the interior of the mini-book, or you can write a sentence with what they have learned from the week for them on the inside of the mini-book. Once the students are done, have them glue the booklet into the mini-lapbook.

📁 **Overall Lapbook** – Have the students cut out the "My Chemistry Projects" pocket on LT p. 15. Have them glue the pocket into the lapbook and add the coloring project they did to the pocket.

Week 2: Mixture

2-Days-a-Week Schedule		
	Day 1	**Day 2**
Read	❑ Read the introduction with the students ❑ Read the selected pages in *The Usborne Children's Encyclopedia*	❑ Choose one or more of the additional books to read from this week
Do	❑ Complete the Scientific Demonstration "Dilution Chemistry" ❑ Eat "Make pudding" for snack	❑ Complete the Nature Study "Muddy Mixtures" ❑ Do the "Diluted Art" activity
Write	❑ Color the main idea page ❑ Fill out the demonstration sheet	❑ Fill out the nature journal sheet ❑ Complete the art page

5-Days-a-Week Schedule					
	Day 1	**Day 2**	**Day 3**	**Day 4**	**Day 5**
Read	❑ Read the introduction with the students	❑ Read the selected pages in *The Usborne Children's Encyclopedia*	❑ Choose one or more of the additional books to read from this week	❑ Choose one or more of the additional books to read from this week	
Do	❑ Eat "Make Pudding" for snack	❑ Complete the Scientific Demonstration "Dilution Chemistry"	❑ Work on the activity "Strongest to Weakest"	❑ Do the "Diluted Art" activity	❑ Complete the Nature Study "Muddy Mixtures"
Write	❑ Color the main idea page	❑ Fill out the demonstration sheet	❑ Complete the Mixtures Mini-book	❑ Complete the art page	❑ Fill out the nature journal sheet

Read – Information Gathering

Weekly Topic

⤷ Adding water to a mixture will make it thinner or weaker.

Scripted Introduction

Have some thick paint on a plate, a paintbrush, and a cup of water in front of each student.

Say to the students:

> This paint is really thick; isn't it? Why don't you try using this to paint over the gray line on the top of the paper.

Let the students paint a line on SD p. 13 with the thick paint on the paper. Then say:

> Now, I am going to add a little water from this cup to our paint mixture. Let's see what happens!

Add the water and let the students use the paint brush to mix the paint and water.

Then ask the students:

> **?** What happened to the paint?

> That's a great description. The paint did get thinner! The scientific word for this is "diluted." We diluted the paint with water to make it thinner. This week, we are going to look closer at mixtures and dilutions. But before we do that, why don't you use our diluted paint mixture to paint over the other gray line on the bottom of the paper?

Read–Alouds

Encyclopedia Pages

📖 *The Usborne Children's Encyclopedia* – There are no new pages scheduled. If you would like, you can reread the pages (pp. 188-189) on solids, liquids, and gases.

Library Books to Look For

📖 *Liquids* (States of Matter) by Carol Ryback and Jim Mezzanotte
📖 *Lulu's Lemonade* (Math Matters) by Barbara Derubertis and Paige Billin-Frye

Do – Hands-on Projects

Scientific Demonstration: Dilution Chemistry

Materials Needed

✓ Juice (whatever juice the students like)

✓ Measuring cups
✓ 5 Cups
✓ Water

Steps to Complete

1. Read the following introduction to your students:

   Remember earlier we saw what happens when we add water to paint? Now, we are going to add water to juice and taste what happens!

2. Lay out five cups in a row and label them 1 to 5.

3. Help the students pour 1 cup of juice into cup 1. Have them pour ¾ cup of juice into cup 2. Have them pour ½ cup of juice into cup 3. Have them pour ¼ cup of juice into cup 4.

4. Then, add ¼ cup of water to cup 2. Add ½ cup of water to cup 3. Add ¾ cup of water to cup 4. Add 1 cup of water to cup 5.

5. Mix all five cups well. Then, have the students drink some of the juice from each cup and rate the juice taste from 1 to 10. When they are done, ask them:

   ? Which cup tasted the strongest?

Explanation

Read the following explaination to the students:

The juice taste got weaker and weaker with the more water we put in the cup. This is because we diluted the juice in the cups with water, like we did with the paint earlier.

Nature Study: Muddy Mixtures

This week, you are looking at mixtures, and mud is a naturally occurring mixture! You don't need a mud puddle. Instead, you will examine the dirt, a.k.a. soil, from outside and then use that soil to make a muddy mixture.

Preparation

✍ To learn more about soil, read pp. 760-764 in the *Handbook of Nature Study* to learn more about soil.

Outdoor Time

✿ Go on a walk with the students to collect some soil. Observe the soil and then use that soil to make your own mud mixture. You can do this by using different amounts of water to get different thicknesses of mud. Allow the students to make their own observations about the soil and the mud you made. You can use the information you have learned from reading the *Handbook of Nature Study* to answer their questions or to share information about soil and mud.

Coordinating Activities

- ✂ **Art** – (Diluted Art) Give the students a plate with one color of paint and plenty of white paint. Have the students paint first with the original color on a piece of paper. Then, have the students dilute their color with the white paint, making sure to paint with each lighter color as they go along.

- ✂ **Snack** – (Make Pudding) Point out to the students that pudding is a mixture. Make pudding together by following the directions found on your pudding package. Before you put the mixture in the fridge, remove ¼ cup of the mixture and put it in another bowl. Add an additional ½ cup of milk to that mixture to dilute it, then put both bowls in the fridge. Check the two bowls after two hours, and see how they differ.

- ✂ **Activity** – (Strongest to Weakest) Make a batch of Kool-Aid or other powdered drink mix. Dilute the drink mix to varying strengths. Have the students do a blind taste test and classify them from strongest to weakest.

Write – Simple Notebooking

Student Diary

- ☐ **Main Idea Page** – Have the students color the coloring page found on SD p. 13.
- ☐ **Demonstration Sheet** – After you do the demonstration, fill out the demonstration sheet found on SD p. 14 with the students.
- ☐ **Nature Journal Sheet** – After you have your nature study time, fill out the nature journal sheet found on SD p. 15 with the students. The students can sketch what they have seen, or you can write down their observations.
- ☐ **Art Page** – Have the students use SD p. 16 to complete the art activity.

Lapbooking Templates

- 📁 **Weekly Mini-book** – Have the students cut out and color the Mixtures Mini-book on LT p. 10. You can have them cut out the main idea graphic included and glue it in the interior of the mini-book, or you can write a sentence with what they have learned from the week for them on the inside of the mini-book. Once the students are done, have them glue the booklet into the mini-lapbook.

- 📁 **Overall Lapbook** – Have the students add the page they painted to the "My Chemistry Projects" pocket in the lapbook.

Week 3: Density

2-Days-a-Week Schedule		
	Day 1	**Day 2**
Read	❏ Read the introduction with the students ❏ Read the selected pages in *The Usborne Children's Encyclopedia*	❏ Choose one or more of the additional books to read from this week
Do	❏ Complete the Scientific Demonstration "Floating" ❏ Eat "Density in Food" for snack	❏ Complete the Nature Study "Density in Nature" ❏ Do the "Marbled Art" activity
Write	❏ Color the main idea page ❏ Fill out the demonstration sheet	❏ Fill out the nature journal sheet ❏ Complete the art page

5-Days-a-Week Schedule					
	Day 1	**Day 2**	**Day 3**	**Day 4**	**Day 5**
Read	❏ Read the introduction with the students	❏ Read the selected pages in *The Usborne Children's Encyclopedia*	❏ Choose one or more of the additional books to read from this week	❏ Choose one or more of the additional books to read from this week	
Do	❏ Eat "Density in Food" for snack	❏ Complete the Scientific Demonstration "Floating"	❏ Work on the activity "Density Fireworks"	❏ Do the "Marbled Art" activity	❏ Complete the Nature Study "Density in Nature"
Write	❏ Color the main idea page	❏ Fill out the demonstration sheet	❏ Complete the Density Mini-book	❏ Complete the art page	❏ Fill out the nature journal sheet

Read – Information Gathering

Weekly Topic

- Oil is less dense than water.

Scripted Introduction

Have a large glass jar with half of a cup of water, a spoon. and half of a cup of oil on a table in front of you. Say to the students:

> We are going to see if we can float this oil on top of the water here in this jar. Here, you hold this spoon over the jar, while I pour the oil on it.

Be sure to pour the oil slowly into the jar to prevent mixing; this way the oil will really float on the water. After you finish pouring about half a cup of oil, ask:

> **?** What's happening? Is the oil sinking to the bottom or floating on top of the water?

> That's right, the oil is floating on top of the water. This is because of density!

> Density tells us how much space an object takes up compared to how much stuff in is the object. The stuff in the oil is not as closely packed together compared to the stuff in the water. In chemistry, we say that oil is less dense than water.

> This week, we are going to take a closer look at density.

Read–Alouds

Encyclopedia Pages

- *The Usborne Children's Encyclopedia* pp. 200-201 "Floating"

Library Books to Look For

- *What Is Density?* (Rookie Read-About Science) by Joanne Barkan
- *Will It Float or Sink?* (Rookie Read-About Science) by Melissa Stewart

Do – Hands-on Projects

Scientific Demonstration: Floating

Materials Needed
- ✓ Glass jar
- ✓ Water

✓ Objects to test, such as cork, apple slice, paper clip, grape, piece of candle, small rubber eraser, spoon, pencil, paper

Steps to Complete

1. Read the following introduction to your students:

   Remember earlier we saw that oil sits on top of water, and that this is because of something we call density? Now, we are going to see how other objects fair in water. We are going to drop them in and observe if they sink or float!

2. Fill the jar about halfway with water, while the students collect six to ten objects to test.

3. Then, let the students drop the objects and observe what happens. When they are done, ask them:

   ? Which objects sank? Which objects float?

Explanation

Read the following explaination to the students:

We saw that some objects sank and some floated in the water. This is because some objects, like a cork, are less dense than water—like oil. These objects will float. On the other hand, some objects, like a paper clip, are more dense that water. These objects will sink.

Nature Study: Density in Nature

This week, you are looking at density, and objects found in nature also have density. So, for your nature study this week, you will find objects and test their density.

Preparation

✐ Make sure that you have access to a bucket of water or a pond for testing.

Outdoor Time

☼ Go on a walk with the students to collect five different objects, such as a leaf, an acorn, a berry, a stick, and a rock. Observe the objects and arrange them in order from lightest to heaviest. Then, drop each object in a bucket of water or pond to see if it sinks or floats.

Coordinating Activities

✂ Art – (Marbled Paper) Powdered chalk is less dense than water and will float. Begin by grating several colors of chalk over a 9x13 pan filled with water. Then, gently swirl the colors and place a piece of paper on the top of the water. Pull the paper out and set it on some paper towels to dry. (*The chalk will transfer to the paper, making your piece of paper appear to be marbled.*)

✂ Snack – (Density in Food) Have several types of fruit set out, such as an apple, a grape, an orange, a pear, or a banana. Have the students examine each fruit and observe how tightly packed the fruit pieces seem. Guide them through rating which fruit is most dense down to which is the least dense. Eat them in order to see if you're correct!

✂ Activity – (Density Fireworks) Do another demonstration that looks at how food coloring bubbles float from oil to water. You will need a glass jar, oil, water, and food coloring. You can find the directions here:

🖰 https://elementalscience.com/blogs/science-activities/kitchen-fireworks

Write – Simple Notebooking

Student Diary

☐ Main Idea Page – Have the students color the coloring page found on SD p. 17.

☐ Demonstration Sheet – After you do the demonstration, fill out the demonstration sheet found on SD p. 18 with the students.

☐ Nature Journal Sheet – After you have your nature study time, fill out the nature journal sheet found on SD p. 19 with the students. The students can sketch the objects on the chart or write the names. Then, have them add a check under the column showing if the object sinks or floats.

☐ Art Page – Once the paper is dry, have the students cut out a piece of it and glue it onto the sheet found on SD p. 20.

Lapbooking Templates

📁 Weekly Mini-book – Have the students cut out and color the Density Mini-book on LT p. 11. You can have them cut out the main idea graphic included and glue it in the interior of the mini-book, or you can write a sentence with what they have learned from the week for them on the inside of the mini-book. Once the students are done, have them glue the booklet into the mini-lapbook.

📁 Overall Lapbook – Have the students add the marbled page to the "My Chemistry Projects" pocket in the lapbook.

Week 4: Crystals

	2-Days-a-Week Schedule	
	Day 1	**Day 2**
Read	❑ Read the introduction with the students ❑ Read the selected pages in *The Usborne Children's Encyclopedia*	❑ Choose one or more of the additional books to read from this week
Do	❑ Complete the Scientific Demonstration "Crystals" ❑ Eat "Edible Crystals" for snack	❑ Complete the Nature Study "Quartz" ❑ Do the "Painting with Crystals" activity
Write	❑ Color the main idea page ❑ Fill out the demonstration sheet	❑ Fill out the nature journal sheet ❑ Complete the art page

	5-Days-a-Week Schedule				
	Day 1	**Day 2**	**Day 3**	**Day 4**	**Day 5**
Read	❑ Read the introduction with the students	❑ Read the selected pages in *The Usborne Children's Encyclopedia*	❑ Choose one or more of the additional books to read from this week	❑ Choose one or more of the additional books to read from this week	
Do	❑ Eat "Edible Crystals" for snack	❑ Complete the Scientific Demonstration "Crystals"	❑ Work on the activity "Crystal Hunt"	❑ Do the "Painting with Crystals" activity	❑ Complete the Nature Study "Quartz"
Write	❑ Color the main idea page	❑ Fill out the demonstration sheet	❑ Complete the Crystal Mini-book	❑ Complete the art page	❑ Fill out the nature journal sheet

Read – Information Gathering

Weekly Topic

- Crystals are made up of minerals found in the Earth.

Scripted Introduction

Have pictures of various types of crystals from books and magazines (or have several rocks with crystals) on the table in front of you. Say to the students:

> This week, we are going to look closer at crystals. These pictures are of (rocks have) crystals.

> **?** What do you notice about crystals?

Give them time to observe the pictures (or rocks) before you say:

> Those are some good observations. Crystals are formed from minerals found in the Earth. They are found in salt, quartz, mica, and so many other types of rocks. This week, we are going to look at and grow our own crystals!

Read-Alouds

Encyclopedia Pages

- *The Usborne Children's Encyclopedia* – There are no new pages scheduled.

Library Books to Look For

- *Crystals (The Golden Science Close-up Series)* by Robert A. Bell
- *Rock and Minerals (Eye Wonder)* by DK Publishing

Do – Hands-on Projects

Scientific Demonstration: Crystals

Materials Needed

- ✓ Plastic bowl (or disposable pie pan)
- ✓ Sponge (cut into 1-inch cubes)
- ✓ Water
- ✓ Salt
- ✓ Liquid bluing
- ✓ Ammonia
- ✓ Measuring spoons

Steps to Complete

Note—*This demonstration will take place over four days, so you will need to set aside the time to check it daily throughout the week.*

1. Read the following introduction to your students:

Remember earlier we looked at some pictures of crystals? Now, we are going to make our own!

2. On day one, have the students place the sponge cubes in the bottom of the bowl. Mix together 2 TBSP each of water, salt, and liquid bluing, and pour the mixture over the sponge cubes. Set the bowl where it won't be disturbed but will still have good air flow.

3. On day two, have the students sprinkle two more tablespoons of salt over the sponges.

4. On day three, pour 2 TBSP each of water, salt, ammonia, and liquid bluing into the bowl, but not directly over the sponge cubes. (*Crystal formations should be beginning to appear on this day*.)

5. On day four, let the students observe what has happened. Ask them:

   ? What do you see?

Explanation

Read the following explaination to the students:

How cool are the crystals that formed on the sponge cubes? If we leave the cubes to sit undisturbed for several more days, we might see even more crystals form.

Nature Study: Quartz

This week, you are looking for a natually occuring crystal: quartz. If quartz is not easy to find in your area, have a piece on hand to observe.

Preparation

⟁ Read pp. 754-755 in the *Handbook of Nature Study* to learn more about quartz.

Outdoor Time

☼ Go on a walk with the students to see if you can find any quartz. Allow the students to observe the quartz rocks they find and ask any questions they may have. You can use the information you have learned from reading the *Handbook of Nature Study* to answer their questions or to share information about what they are observing.

Coordinating Activities

✂ Art – (Painting with Crystals) Have the students paint with a crystal solution that evaporates leaving behind snowflake-like crystals. You will need Epsom salts, warm water, a glass, food coloring (blue is best), and a paintbrush. See the directions for this activity here:

   ⌦ https://elementalscience.com/blogs/science-activities/how-to-paint-crystal-snowflakes-epsom-salts

✂ Snack – (Edible Crystals) Set out two small bowls of sugar and salt. Let the students use their five senses to observe more about the two. Allow them to use a magnifying glass to look closer at the crystals. Explain to the students that these are two crystals that we can eat. (*Be sure to remind the studentss that not all crystals are safe to eat and they should always ask you before trying to eat any kind of crystals.*)

✂ Activity – (Crystal Hunt) Take a walk around your house and see what crystals you can find. You can look for things like crystals in jewelry, rock collections, pictures, magazines, and even in the kitchen.

Write – Simple Notebooking

Student Diary

☐ Main Idea Page – Have the students color the coloring page found on SD p. 21.

☐ Demonstration Sheet – After you do the demonstration, fill out the demonstration sheet found on SD p. 22 with the students.

☐ Nature Journal Sheet – After you have your nature study time, fill out the nature journal sheet found on SD p. 23 with the students. The students can sketch what they have seen, or you can write down their observations.

☐ Art Page – Have the students use SD p. 24 to complete the art activity.

Lapbooking Templates

📁 Weekly Mini-book – Have the students cut out and color the Crystal Mini-book on LT p. 12. You can have them cut out the main idea graphic included and glue it in the interior of the mini-book, or you can write a sentence with what they have learned from the week for them on the inside of the mini-book. Once the students are done, have them glue the booklet into the mini-lapbook.

📁 Overall Lapbook – Have the students add the page with their sparkling rocks to the "My Chemistry Projects" pocket in the lapbook.

Week 5: Colors

2-Days-a-Week Schedule		
	Day 1	**Day 2**
Read	❑ Read the introduction with the students ❑ Read the selected pages in *The Usborne Children's Encyclopedia*	❑ Choose one or more of the additional books to read from this week
Do	❑ Complete the Scientific Demonstration "Color Mixing" ❑ Eat "Color Cookies" for snack	❑ Complete the Nature Study "Color in Nature" ❑ Do the "Color Painting" activity
Write	❑ Color the main idea page ❑ Fill out the demonstration sheet	❑ Fill out the nature journal sheet ❑ Complete the art page

5-Days-a-Week Schedule					
	Day 1	**Day 2**	**Day 3**	**Day 4**	**Day 5**
Read	❑ Read the introduction with the students	❑ Read the selected pages in *The Usborne Children's Encyclopedia*	❑ Choose one or more of the additional books to read from this week	❑ Choose one or more of the additional books to read from this week	
Do	❑ Eat "Color Cookies" for snack	❑ Complete the Scientific Demonstration "Color Mixing"	❑ Work on the activity "Making Rainbows"	❑ Do the "Color Painting" activity	❑ Complete the Nature Study "Color in Nature"
Write	❑ Color the main idea page	❑ Fill out the demonstration sheet	❑ Complete the Colors Mini-book	❑ Complete the art page	❑ Fill out the nature journal sheet

Read – Information Gathering

Weekly Topic

- Two colors can be mixed to make a new color.

Scripted Introduction

Have three clear glasses, one half filled with yellow water, one half filled with blue water, and one empty on the table in front of you. Say to the students:

> In front of me are two glasses with different-colored water and one empty glass. Both yellow and blue are primary colors. Let's be color chemists and see what happens when we pour the two colors into the empty glass.

You can pour both or let the students do the pouring. Either way, when you are done ask the students:

> **?** What color did we make?

> That's right, green is a secondary color because it is made by mixing two primary colors. We mixed yellow and blue to make a new color, green. This week, we are going look at what happens when we mix colors.

You may want to also introduce the color wheel and rainbows at this time.

Read–Alouds

Encyclopedia Pages

- *The Usborne Children's Encyclopedia* pp. 206-207 "Light and Color"

Library Books to Look For

- *All the Colors of the Rainbow* (Rookie Read-About Science) by Allan Fowler
- *The Magic School Bus Makes A Rainbow: A Book About Color* by Joanna Cole
- *I Love Colors!* (Hello Reader!, Level 1) by Hans Wilhelm

Do – Hands-on Projects

Scientific Demonstration: Color Mixing

Materials Needed

- ✓ 4 Clear glasses
- ✓ Eyedropper
- ✓ Food coloring (red, yellow, blue)
- ✓ Water

Steps to Complete

1. Read the following introduction to your students:

   Remember earlier we mixed yellow water and blue water and it turned green? We are going to continue our test, only this time we are going to use all three of the primary colors!

2. Fill three of the cups about halfway with water. Add several drops of red food coloring to one, several drops of yellow food coloring to another, and several drops of blue food coloring to the remaining cup with water. Mix each of the cups well.

3. Have the students use the eyedropper to suck up one of the colors and add it to the empty cup. Then, have them choose another one of the primary colors to suck up and add to the first color they added. Mix well and ask them:

   ? What color did you create?

   Empty and rinse the cup you used to mix the colors.

4. Next, repeat the process with the remaining colors until they have mixed red and yellow, yellow and blue, and blue and red.

5. Then, let them explore mixing colors, adding whatever they want!

Explanation

Read the following explaination to the students:

We saw earlier that when you mix yellow and blue, it creates the secondary color green. Today, we saw that when you mix red and yellow, it creates the secondary color orange. And we saw that when you mix red and blue, it creates the secondary color purple. Then, when we mix all the colors together, we get black—how cool is that?

Nature Study: Colors in Nature

This week, you are looking at colors and how they mix to form new colors. Rainbows are good examples of primary and secondary colors in nature, so this week your nature study time will focus on that.

Preparation

⚘ Have a prism on hand in case you don't find a rainbow.

Outdoor Time

✿ Go on a walk with the students to see if you can find a rainbow. If you're lucky enough to see one in the sky, allow the students to make their own observations and then sketch the rainbow in their nature journal. If not, look at the edges of the clouds for rainbows, or find a sunny spot and use a prism to create a rainbow on a sidewalk.

Coordinating Activities

- ✂ Art – (Color Painting) Give each student a paper plate with a little red, yellow, and blue paint on it. Have them mix the colors to make orange, green, and purple. Then, let them paint their own rainbow.

- ✂ Snack – (Color Cookies) Make sugar cookies using your favorite recipe, or purchase them from the store. Give the students several bowls with a little bit of white icing in each. Let them choose which colors to add to their icing. Then decorate the cookies with the different colors they created.

- ✂ Activity – (Making Rainbows) Pour milk in a bowl. Place three drops of red, yellow, and blue food coloring in three different places in the bowl. Add a drop of liquid dish soap, and watch the colors mix.

Write – Simple Notebooking

Student Diary

- ☐ Main Idea Page – Have the students color the beakers with the colors they observed on the coloring page found on SD p. 25.

- ☐ Demonstration Sheet – After you do the demonstration, fill out the demonstration sheet found on SD p. 26 with the students.

- ☐ Nature Journal Sheet – After you have your nature study time, fill out the nature journal sheet found on SD p. 27 with the students. The students can sketch what they have seen, or you can write down their observations.

- ☐ Art Page – Have the students use SD p. 28 to complete the art activity.

Lapbooking Templates

- 📁 Weekly Mini-book – Have the students cut out and color the Colors Mini-book on LT p. 13. You can have them cut out the main idea graphic included and glue it in the interior of the mini-book, or you can write a sentence with what they have learned from the week for them on the inside of the mini-book. Once the students are done, have them glue the booklet into the mini-lapbook.

- 📁 Overall Lapbook – Have the students add the page they painted to the "My Chemistry Projects" pocket in the lapbook.

Week 6: Freezing

2-Days-a-Week Schedule		
	Day 1	**Day 2**
Read	❏ Read the introduction with the students ❏ Read the selected pages in *The Usborne Children's Encyclopedia*	❏ Choose one or more of the additional books to read from this week
Do	❏ Complete the Scientific Demonstration "Freezing" ❏ Eat "Frozen Foods" for snack	❏ Complete the Nature Study "Weather Observation" ❏ Do the "Ice Painting" activity
Write	❏ Color the main idea page ❏ Fill out the demonstration sheet	❏ Fill out the nature journal sheet ❏ Complete the art page

5-Days-a-Week Schedule					
	Day 1	**Day 2**	**Day 3**	**Day 4**	**Day 5**
Read	❏ Read the introduction with the students	❏ Read the selected pages in *The Usborne Children's Encyclopedia*	❏ Choose one or more of the additional books to read from this week	❏ Choose one or more of the additional books to read from this week	
Do	❏ Eat "Frozen Foods" for snack	❏ Complete the Scientific Demonstration "Freezing"	❏ Work on the activity "Freeze Tag"	❏ Do the "Ice Painting" activity	❏ Complete the Nature Study "Weather Observation"
Write	❏ Color the main idea page	❏ Fill out the demonstration sheet	❏ Complete the Freezing Mini-book	❏ Complete the art page	❏ Fill out the nature journal sheet

Read – Information Gathering

Weekly Topic

- When water freezes, it changes into ice.

Scripted Introduction

Have a few cubes of ice on a plate on the table in front of you. Say to the students:

Did you know that ice is really water? When water freezes, it changes into ice. Today, we are going to make some observations about ice.

Ask the students the following questions as they observe the piece of ice:

? How does the ice feel?

? How does the ice smell?

? What color is the piece of ice?

Let the students touch and observe the ice before saying the following:

When water freezes, it changes into ice, but as you can see, when ice melts it turns back into water! This week, we are going to learn about freezing.

Read-Alouds

Encyclopedia Pages

- *The Usborne Children's Encyclopedia* pp. 190-191 "How materials change"

Library Books to Look For

- *Freezing and Melting* (First Step Nonfiction) by Robin Nelson
- *Solids, Liquids, And Gases* (Rookie Read-About Science) by Ginger Garrett

Do – Hands-on Projects

Scientific Demonstration: Freezing

Materials Needed

- ✓ Ice cube tray (or small plastic containers)
- ✓ Various household liquids (i.e., water, milk, liquid soap, oil, ketchup, honey, or mustard)

Steps to Complete

1. Read the following introduction to your students:

Remember earlier we observed frozen water? It was cold and hard; wasn't it?

Now, we are going to see what happens when we try to freeze other liquids that we can find in our house!

2. Have the students select at least six different liquids to attempt to freeze.

3. Have them add the liquids to the ice cube tray (or small plastic containers). Place the tray into the freezer.

4. Have the students check the tray after an hour to observe what happens to the liquids.

? What has happened to the liquids?

Explanation

The results for this demonstration will vary depending on the liquids the students chose. Be sure to recap what froze and what didn't.

Nature Study: Weather Observation

This week, you will be observing the weather.

Preparation

↻ Read pp. 808-814 in the *Handbook of Nature Study* to learn more about water's forms and how they relate to weather.

Outdoor Time

☼ Go on a walk and observe the weather. Allow the students to make more observations about the weather they see. If they need some help, ask them are there clouds in the sky? If so, what color are they? What is the temperature like today? Talk to the students about how water (rain) falls from the sky. Also explain that when the temperature is cold enough, frozen water falls from the sky and we call that snow.

Coordinating Activities

✂ Art – (Ice Painting) Ahead of time, use food coloring to make several different colors of water, and then freeze the colored water into cubes. Once the cubes are frozen, let the students paint with the ice.

✂ Snack – (Frozen Foods) Ahead of time, freeze some of the students' favorite fruits or vegetables (i.e., peas, corn, carrots, grapes, strawberries, or bananas—you could also freeze their favorite cookies or crackers). Serve the frozen food for snack. Have the students taste each one and talk about how it tastes the same and how it tastes different.

✂ Activity – (Freeze Tag) Have the students play a game of freeze tag. To add in melting to the game, have the tagged players shout "freeze" the first time they are tagged and "melt" when they are tagged a second time to be unfrozen.

Write – Simple Notebooking

Student Diary

- ☐ **Main Idea Page** – Have the students color the coloring page found on SD p. 29.
- ☐ **Demonstration Sheet** – After you do the demonstration, fill out the demonstration sheet found on SD p. 30 with the students.
- ☐ **Nature Journal Sheet** – After you have your nature study time, fill out the nature journal sheet found on SD p. 31 with the students. The students can sketch what they have seen, or you can write down their observations.
- ☐ **Art Page** – Have the students use SD p. 32 to complete the art activity.

Lapbooking Templates

- 🗀 **Weekly Mini-book** – Have the students cut out and color the Freezing Mini-book on LT p. 14. You can have them cut out the main idea graphic included and glue it in the interior of the mini-book, or you can write a sentence with what they have learned from the week for them on the inside of the mini-book. Once the students are done, have them glue the booklet into the mini-lapbook.
- 🗀 **Overall Lapbook** – Have the students add the page they painted to the "My Chemistry Projects" pocket in the lapbook.

Intro to Science

Unit 2: Intro to Physics

Intro to Physics Unit Overview

Sequence for Study

- 🌍 Week 1: Force
- 🌍 Week 2: Gravity
- 🌍 Week 3: Magnets
- 🌍 Week 4: Inclined Planes
- 🌍 Week 5: Sound
- 🌍 Week 6: Light

Supplies Needed for the Unit

Week	Introduction Props	Hands-on Project Materials	Coordinating Activities Supplies
1	Marble	Toy car, String (2 feet long), Tape	Paint, Paintbrush, Cutting board, Different kinds of round fruits and vegetables, Several rubber bands, Measuring tape
2	Pencil	Several objects of varying size and weight (crayon, pompom, paper, balloon, paper clip, and more)	Apple, Balloons, Paper, Eyedropper, Paint
3	Bar magnet, Several metal paper clips	String, Magnet, Variety of metal and nonmetal objects	Sugar cookie, Red and blue M&M's, Paper, Thin cardboard, Paint, Several magnetic objects, Magnet
4	Long wooden block, Toy car	Marble, Bouncy ball, Thin wooden board or thick cardboard, Blocks, Tape (or other marker)	Graham crackers, Marshmallows, Bowl of water, Eye dropper, Wax paper, Marbles, Plate, Paint, Block, Paper, Thin cardboard
5	(No supplies needed.)	An empty yogurt container, Wax paper, Rubber band, Salt, Sound makers	2 Paper plates, Paint, Tape, Beans, Rice Krispies cereal, Bowl, Milk, Toilet paper tube
6	(No supplies needed.)	Bubble solution and wand, Plate	Flashlights, Reflective materials, Paper, Glue

Books Scheduled

Hands-on Projects

📖 *Handbook of Nature Study (If you are using the nature study option.)*

Scheduled Encylopedias

📖 *The Usborne Children's Encyclopedia*

Library Books to Look For

Optional Encyclopedia

📖 *The Usborne Children's Encyclopedia*

Week 1

📖 *Ways Things Move (First Step Nonfiction)* by Robin Nelson

📖 *Energy in Motion (Rookie Read-About Science)* by Melissa Stewart

📖 *Move It!: Motion, Forces and You* by Adrienne Mason and Claudia Davila

📖 *Forces & Motion (Little Science Stars)* by Clint Twist

Week 2

📖 *Gravity Is a Mystery* (Let's-Read-and-Find... Science 2) by Franklyn M. Branley

📖 *What Is Gravity?* (Rookie Read-About Science) by Lisa Trumbauer

📖 *Gravity* (Blastoff! Readers: First Science) by Kay Manolis

📖 *Galileo's Leaning Tower Experiment* (Junior Library Guild Selection) by Wendy Macdonald

Week 3

📖 *Magnets* (All Aboard Science Reader) by Anne Schreiber and Adrian C. Sinnott

📖 *What Makes a Magnet?* (Let's-Read-and-Find... Science 2) by Franklyn M. Branley and True Kelley

📖 *Magnets: Pulling Together, Pushing Apart* (Amazing Science) by Natalie M. Boyd

Week 4

📖 *Inclined Planes to the Rescue* (First Facts) by Thales and Sharon

📖 *Inclined Planes and Wedges* (Early Bird Physics Series) by Sally M. Walker

📖 *What are Inclined Planes?* (Looking at Simple Machines) by Helen Frost

Week 5

📖 *Sound Waves (Energy in Action)* by Ian F. Mahaney

📖 *Oscar and the Bat: A Book About Sound (Start with Science)* by Geoff Waring

📖 *Sounds All Around (Let's-Read-and-Find... Science 1)* by Wendy Pfeffer and Holly Keller

📖 *All about Sound (Rookie Read-About Science)* by Lisa Trumbauer

Week 6

📖 *All About Light* (Rookie Read-About Science) by Lisa Trumbauer

📖 *Exploring Light* (How Does Science Work?) by Carol Ballard

📖 *The Magic School Bus: Gets A Bright Idea, The: A Book About Light* by Nancy White

Week 1: Force

2-Days-a-Week Schedule		
	Day 1	**Day 2**
Read	❏ Read the introduction with the students ❏ Read the selected pages in *The Usborne Children's Encyclopedia*	❏ Choose one or more of the additional books to read from this week
Do	❏ Complete the Scientific Demonstration "Push and Pull" ❏ Eat "Food in Motion" for snack	❏ Complete the Nature Study "Weather Observation" ❏ Do the "Motion Painting" activity
Write	❏ Color the main idea page ❏ Fill out the demonstration sheet	❏ Fill out the nature journal sheet ❏ Complete the art page

5-Days-a-Week Schedule					
	Day 1	**Day 2**	**Day 3**	**Day 4**	**Day 5**
Read	❏ Read the introduction with the students	❏ Read the selected pages in *The Usborne Children's Encyclopedia*	❏ Choose one or more of the additional books to read from this week	❏ Choose one or more of the additional books to read from this week	
Do	❏ Eat "Food in Motion" for snack	❏ Complete the Scientific Demonstration "Push and Pull"	❏ Work on the activity "Energy Race"	❏ Do the "Motion Painting" activity	❏ Complete the Nature Study "Weather Observation"
Write	❏ Color the main idea page	❏ Fill out the demonstration sheet	❏ Complete the Forces Mini-book	❏ Complete the art page	❏ Fill out the nature journal sheet

Read – Information Gathering

Weekly Topic

- A force is a push or a pull that can cause motion or slow it down.

Scripted Introduction

Set a marble on the table so that it sits still and doesn't move. Say to the students:

> When this marble is sitting on the flat surface of the table, it doesn't move. But what happens if we bump the table?

Gently bump the table. Ask the students:

> **?** What happened?

> You're right! The marble moved, even though we didn't touch it.

> The bump to the table caused the table to move a bit. The movement of the table caused the marble to wobble.

> In science, we call this transfer of a push or a pull force. This week, we are going to spend some time learning about forces.

Read-Alouds

Encyclopedia Pages

- *The Usborne Children's Encyclopedia* pp. 194-195 "Forces"

Library Books to Look For

- *Ways Things Move (First Step Nonfiction)* by Robin Nelson
- *Energy in Motion (Rookie Read-About Science)* by Melissa Stewart
- *Move It!: Motion, Forces and You* by Adrienne Mason and Claudia Davila
- *Forces & Motion (Little Science Stars)* by Clint Twist

Do – Hands-on Projects

Scientific Demonstration: Push and Pull

Materials Needed

- ✓ Toy car
- ✓ String (2 feet long)
- ✓ Tape

Steps to Complete

1. Read the following introduction to your students:

   Remember earlier we saw the marble move without touching it? This was because of a force. Now, we are going to test out some push and pull forces on a toy car!

2. Place the toy car on the table in front of the students. Ask the students:

   ? Is the car moving or standing still?

3. Have the students push the car gently. Ask the students:

   ? What happened to the car this time?

4. Have the students tape the string to the front of the car. Have them hold the other end and pull gently. Ask the students:

   ? What happened to the car this time?

5. Let the students continue to use forces, pushes and pulls, to move the car around the table.

Explanation

   Read the following explaination to the students:

   We saw the car stood still until a force was applied. The push force caused the car to move and so did the pull force from the string. The car continues to move until the force of friction slows it down.

Nature Study: Weather Observation

   This week, you are studying forces, many of which can be observed in nature through things like wind and water. For your nature study this week, you will do another weather observation, but this time you will be specifically looking for signs of movement caused by wind.

Preparation

   ⟁ Read pp. 791-798 in the *Handbook of Nature Study* to learn more about winds.

Outdoor Time

   ☼ Go on a walk to look for signs of movement in nature. You can look for how the wind blows through the trees or other evidence of a breeze. Discuss what you see using the information you have learned from reading the *Handbook of Nature Study* to answer their questions or to share information about what they are observing.

Coordinating Activities

   ✂ Art – (Motion Painting) Have the students paint a picture using motion. You will need paint, a paintbrush, and paper. Have the students dip the paintbrush in the paint and then set it on the paper. Have them pick the paintbrush up and observe the mark. Then, have them set the paintbrush in a different spot on the paper and pull the paintbrush to the other side. Repeat this process, only this time have them push the paintbrush. How do the three paintbrush marks differ?

✂ **Snack** – (Food in Motion) Have the students play with their food to learn about motion! Have them roll different fruits and vegetables, such as carrots, blueberries, oranges, grapes, or other round food items, down a cutting board ramp to see which rolls the farthest.

✂ **Activity** – (Energy Race) Have the students compete to see who can use the most force to move to their rubber band. You will need several people, a rubber band for each person, and a measuring tape. Draw a line at one end of a room or outside. Give each player a rubber band and have them stand on the line. Call out "pull," at which point the players will use a pull force to stretch their rubber bands. Then, call out "let go," at which point the players will let go. The pull force will cause the rubber band to fly forward. Measure the distance each rubber band has traveled. The player whose rubber band has traveled the farthest wins the race!

Write – Simple Notebooking

Student Diary

☐ **Main Idea Page** – Have the students color the coloring page found on SD p. 35.

☐ **Demonstration Sheet** – After you do the demonstration, fill out the demonstration sheet found on SD p. 36 with the students.

☐ **Nature Journal Sheet** – After you have your nature study time, fill out the nature journal sheet found on SD p. 37 with the students. The students can sketch what they have seen, or you can write down their observations.

☐ **Art Page** – Have the students use SD p. 38 to complete the art activity.

Lapbooking Templates

📁 **Weekly Mini-book** – Have the students cut out and color the Forces Mini-book on LT p. 19. You can have them cut out the main idea graphic included and glue it in the interior of the mini-book, or you can write a sentence with what they have learned from the week for them on the inside of the mini-book. Once the students are done, have them glue the booklet into the mini-lapbook.

📁 **Overall Lapbook** – Have the students cut out the "My Physics Projects" pocket on LT p. 25. Have them glue the pocket into the lapbook and add the coloring project they did to the pocket.

Week 2: Gravity

You do not need to complete all of this in a week. Instead, choose from the following options.

2-Days-a-Week Schedule		
	Day 1	**Day 2**
Read	❏ Read the introduction with the students ❏ Read the selected pages in *The Usborne Children's Encyclopedia*	❏ Choose one or more of the additional books to read from this week
Do	❏ Complete the Scientific Demonstration "Gravity Pull" ❏ Eat "Gravity Apples" for snack	❏ Complete the Nature Study "Apple Tree" ❏ Do the "Gravity Drops" activity
Write	❏ Color the main idea page ❏ Fill out the demonstration sheet	❏ Fill out the nature journal sheet ❏ Complete the art page

5-Days-a-Week Schedule					
	Day 1	**Day 2**	**Day 3**	**Day 4**	**Day 5**
Read	❏ Read the introduction with the students	❏ Read the selected pages in *The Usborne Children's Encyclopedia*	❏ Choose one or more of the additional books to read from this week	❏ Choose one or more of the additional books to read from this week	
Do	❏ Eat "Gravity Apples" for snack	❏ Complete the Scientific Demonstration "Gravity Pull"	❏ Work on the activity "Gravity Race"	❏ Do the "Gravity Drops" activity	❏ Complete the Nature Study "Apple Tree"
Write	❏ Color the main idea page	❏ Fill out the demonstration sheet	❏ Complete the Gravity Mini-book	❏ Complete the art page	❏ Fill out the nature journal sheet

Read – Information Gathering

Weekly Topic

- Gravity is the force that pulls all things to the ground.

Scripted Introduction

Have a pencil on the table in front of the student. Say to the students:

Watch what happens when I drop this pencil.

Pick up the pencil, hold it at shoulder height, and let go. Then, ask the students:

? What happened to the pencil?

That's right! It fell to the ground. This happened because of gravity.

Gravity is the invisible force that pulls all things to the ground. We can't see it, but it affects us every day. If there were no gravity, we would float up in the air!

This week, we are going to spend some time learning about gravity.

Read-Alouds

Encyclopedia Pages

- *The Usborne Children's Encyclopedia* pp. 198-199 "Gravity"

Library Books to Look For

- *Gravity Is a Mystery* (Let's-Read-and-Find... Science 2) by Franklyn M. Branley and Edward Miller
- *What Is Gravity?* (Rookie Read-About Science) by Lisa Trumbauer
- *Gravity* (Blastoff! Readers: First Science) by Kay Manolis
- *Galileo's Leaning Tower Experiment* (Junior Library Guild Selection) by Wendy Macdonald and Paolo Rui

Do – Hands-on Projects

Scientific Demonstration: Gravity Pull

Materials Needed

- ✓ Several objects of varying size and weight (crayon, pom-pom, paper, balloon, paper clip, and more)

Steps to Complete

1. Read the following introduction to your students:

    Remember earlier we saw that when we let go of the pencil, it dropped to the ground? We found out that this was because of an invisible force called gravity. Now, we are going to see if this invisible force affects everything we drop!

2. Place the collection of objects on the table.

3. Have the students select one and hold it out at shoulder height or a bit higher.

4. Then, have them let go and observe what happens.

5. When they are done, ask them:

    ? What happened to each object when you let go?

Explanation

Read the following explaination to the students:

We saw that all of the objects fell toward the ground when we let go of them. This is because of the invisible force of gravity.

Nature Study: Apple Tree

This week, you are looking at gravity. Isaac Newton discovered gravity when an apple fell on his head. In honor of his discovery, you are going to study the apple tree this week.

Preparation

✎ Read pp. 661-664 in the *Handbook of Nature Study* to learn more about apple trees.

Outdoor Time

☼ Go on a walk with the students to see if you can find an apple trees to observe. Allow the students to observe the tree and ask any questions they may have. You can use the information you have learned from reading the *Handbook of Nature Study* to answer their questions or to share information about what they are observing.

Coordinating Activities

✂ Art – (Gravity Drops) Have the students use gravity to paint a picture. Give them an eye dropper and a paint bottle. Using the eye dropper, have the student draw up some paint and then drop the paint on a piece of paper. The student can do this from various heights, but the higher they drop from, the more the paint will splash!

✂ Snack – (Gravity Apples) Isaac Newton discovered gravity when an apple fell on his head. In honor of his discovery, have apple slices for snack.

✂ Activity – (Gravity Race) You will need a blown-up balloon for this game. Hold the balloon out at arm's length and drop it. Let the balloon hit the ground to show how gravity pulls even the lightest objects toward the ground. Then, explain to the students that they are going to race against gravity to try to keep the balloon up in the air.

Write – Simple Notebooking

Student Diary

- ☐ Main Idea Page – Have the students color the coloring page found on SD p. 39.
- ☐ Demonstration Sheet – After you do the demonstration, fill out the demonstration sheet found on SD p. 40 with the students.
- ☐ Nature Journal Sheet – After you have your nature study time, fill out the nature journal sheet found on SD p. 41 with the students. The students can sketch what they have seen, or you can write down their observations.
- ☐ Art Page – Have the students use SD p. 42 to complete the art activity.

Lapbooking Templates

- 📂 Weekly Mini-book – Have the students cut out and color the Gravity Mini-book on LT p. 20. You can have them cut out the main idea graphic included and glue it in the interior of the mini-book, or you can write a sentence with what they have learned from the week for them on the inside of the mini-book. Once the students are done, have them glue the booklet into the mini-lapbook.
- 📂 Overall Lapbook – Have them add the art project they did to the "My Physics Projects" pocket.

Week 3: Magnets

2-Days-a-Week Schedule		
	Day 1	**Day 2**
Read	❑ Read the introduction with the students ❑ Read the selected pages in *The Usborne Children's Encyclopedia*	❑ Choose one or more of the additional books to read from this week
Do	❑ Complete the Scientific Demonstration "Magnetic Attraction" ❑ Eat "Magnet Cookies" for snack	❑ Complete the Nature Study "Magnetism in Nature" ❑ Do the "Painting with Magnets" activity
Write	❑ Color the main idea page ❑ Fill out the demonstration sheet	❑ Fill out the nature journal sheet ❑ Complete the art page

5-Days-a-Week Schedule					
	Day 1	**Day 2**	**Day 3**	**Day 4**	**Day 5**
Read	❑ Read the introduction with the students	❑ Read the selected pages in *The Usborne Children's Encyclopedia*	❑ Choose one or more of the additional books to read from this week	❑ Choose one or more of the additional books to read from this week	
Do	❑ Eat "Magnet Cookies" for snack	❑ Complete the Scientific Demonstration "Magnetic Attraction"	❑ Work on the activity "Magnetic Household"	❑ Do the "Painting with Magnets" activity	❑ Complete the Nature Study "Magnetism in Nature"
Write	❑ Color the main idea page	❑ Fill out the demonstration sheet	❑ Complete the Magnets Mini-book	❑ Complete the art page	❑ Fill out the nature journal sheet

Read – Information Gathering

Weekly Topic

- Magnets are attracted to certain kinds of metal.

Scripted Introduction

Have a bar magnet and several metal paper clips on the table in front of you. Say to the students:

This is a magnet that can attract metal! Let's see what happens when we put the magnet near these paper clips.

Hover the magnet over the paper clips until one "jumps" up. Then, ask:

? What happened?

That's right! The paper clip jumped up because it was attracted to the magnet. Magnets are attracted to certain kinds of metal. Paper clips are magnetic, which means that they are attracted to magnets.

Let's see how many paper clips this magnet will hold.

Hold up the magnet and let the students add paper clips until the magnet can't hold any more. When they are done, say:

This week, we are going to spend some time learning about magnets.

Read–Alouds

Encyclopedia Pages

The Usborne Children's Encyclopedia pp. 204-205 "Magnets"

Library Books to Look For

- *Magnets* (All Aboard Science Reader) by Anne Schreiber and Adrian C. Sinnott
- *What Makes a Magnet?* (Let's-Read-and-Find... Science 2) by Franklyn M. Branley and True Kelley
- *Magnets: Pulling Together, Pushing Apart* (Amazing Science) by Natalie M. Boyd

Do – Hands-on Projects

Scientific Demonstration: Magnetic Attraction

Materials Needed

- ✓ String

- ✓ Magnet (bar or horseshoe)
- ✓ Variety of metal and nonmetal objects (such as pins, soda cans, coins, cotton, wood, paper, or another magnet)

Steps to Complete

1. Read the following introduction to your students:

   Remember earlier we saw how magnets attracted the paper clip? This was because the paper clip was made from metal and magnets are attraced to metal. Now, we are going to use lots of other objects to see what is attracted to magnets and what is not!

2. Lay the objects out on the table.

3. Have the students use a magnet to try to attract the objects. Let them observe which objects can be picked up by the magnets and which ones cannot.

4. Have them add their observations with your help to the chart on the demonstration sheet.

Explanation

The results will vary with this demonstration. For the explanation, simply recap what you saw.

Nature Study: Magnetism in Nature

This week, you are looking for objects in nature that are magnetic.

Preparation

↻ Read pp. 776-779 in the *Handbook of Nature Study* to learn more about magnets.

Outdoor Time

✿ Go on a walk with the students to collect various objects to test for magnetism. Allow the students to make the choice of what they want to bring home to test, or let them test the materials in the field!

Coordinating Activities

✂ **Art** – (Painting with Magnets) Collect several magnetic objects, such as a metal washer, a metal ball, and a paper clip, for the students to paint with. Use a piece of paper taped onto a thin sheet of cardboard to give the paper some strength. Have the students dip the metal objects in paint and then put them on the paper. Use a magnet from the underside of the paper to drag the object across the paper so that it "paints" on the paper.

✂ **Snack** – (Magnet Cookies) Make your favorite sugar cookie recipe. Use red and blue M&M's to make the design of a magnet on the cookies. Bake and enjoy.

✂ **Activity** – (Magnetic Household) Give the students a magnet, and let them walk around your house testing various objects to see if they are magnetic. (**Note**—*Be sure not to let them use the magnets near computers or other electronics.*)

Write – Simple Notebooking

Student Diary

- [ ] **Main Idea Page** – Have the students color the coloring page found on SD p. 43.
- [ ] **Demonstration Sheet** – After you do the demonstration, fill out the demonstration sheet found on SD p. 44 with the students.
- [ ] **Nature Journal Sheet** – After you have your nature study time, fill out the nature journal sheet found on SD p. 45 with the students. The students can sketch what they have seen, or you can write down their observations.
- [ ] **Art Page** – Have the students use SD p. 46 to complete the art activity.

Lapbooking Templates

- 📁 **Weekly Mini-book** – Have the students cut out and color the Magnet Mini-book on LT p. 21. You can have them cut out the main idea graphic included and glue it in the interior of the mini-book, or you can write a sentence with what they have learned from the week for them on the inside of the mini-book. Once the students are done, have them glue the booklet into the mini-lapbook.
- 📁 **Overall Lapbook** – Have them add the art project they did to the "My Physics Projects" pocket.

Week 4: Inclined Planes

2-Days-a-Week Schedule		
	Day 1	**Day 2**
Read	❑ Read the introduction with the students ❑ Read the selected pages in *The Usborne Children's Encyclopedia*	❑ Choose one or more of the additional books to read from this week
Do	❑ Complete the Scientific Demonstration "Ball Ramp" ❑ Eat "Marshmallow Ramps" for snack	❑ Complete the Nature Study "Ramps in Nature" ❑ Do the "Ramp Painting" activity
Write	❑ Color the main idea page ❑ Fill out the demonstration sheet	❑ Fill out the nature journal sheet ❑ Complete the art page

5-Days-a-Week Schedule					
	Day 1	**Day 2**	**Day 3**	**Day 4**	**Day 5**
Read	❑ Read the introduction with the students	❑ Read the selected pages in *The Usborne Children's Encyclopedia*	❑ Choose one or more of the additional books to read from this week	❑ Choose one or more of the additional books to read from this week	
Do	❑ Eat "Marshmallow Ramps" for snack	❑ Complete the Scientific Demonstration "Ball Ramp"	❑ Work on the activity "Water Droplet Race"	❑ Do the "Ramp Painting" activity	❑ Complete the Nature Study "Ramps in Nature"
Write	❑ Color the main idea page	❑ Fill out the demonstration sheet	❑ Complete the Inclined Planes Mini-book	❑ Complete the art page	❑ Fill out the nature journal sheet

Read – Information Gathering

Weekly Topic

- A ramp is called an inclined plane.

Scripted Introduction

On the table, have a small toy car and a long wooden block set up as an inclined plane, otherwise known as a ramp. Say to the students:

> Remember a few weeks back we leared about forces. We saw that a car sitting on a flat surface doesn't move unless a force pushes or pulls it. Let's see what happens when I put it at the top of the ramp.

Place the car at the top of the wooden block ramp and let go. Ask the students:

> **?** What happened?

> You're right! It rolled down the ramp. We call this ramp an inclined plane, which is a type of simple machine. Inclined planes make it easier for us to take an object up or down by spreading out the height over a distance.

> This week, we are going to spend some time learning about inclined planes.

Read-Alouds

Encyclopedia Pages

- *The Usborne Children's Encyclopedia* – There are no new pages scheduled.

Library Books to Look For

- *Inclined Planes to the Rescue* (First Facts) by Thales and Sharon
- *Inclined Planes and Wedges* (Early Bird Physics Series) by Sally M. Walker
- *What are Inclined Planes?* (Looking at Simple Machines) by Helen Frost

Do – Hands-on Projects

Scientific Demonstration: Ball Ramp

Materials Needed

- ✓ Marble
- ✓ Bouncy ball
- ✓ Thin wooden board or thick cardboard
- ✓ Blocks

✓ Tape (or other marker)

Steps to Complete

1. Read the following introduction to your students:

   Remember earlier we saw how the car rolled down the ramp? This was because the ramp was an inclined plane, which makes it easier for the car to get into motion. Now, we are going to see what happens to several balls as they roll down and inclined plance!

2. Set up a ramp using the blocks and the thin wooden board or thick cardboard.

3. Then, have the students drop the marble at the top of the ramp so that it rolls down. Use the tape to mark where the ball stops. Next, help the students measure how far the tape is from the ramp. Repeat this process two more times.

4. Then, have the students repeat step three with the bouncy ball. When they are done, ask them:

   ? Did the bouncy ball roll further than the marble?

Explanation

Read the following explaination to the students:

We saw that both the balls rolled down the ramp. We also saw that the marble tended to roll farther than the bouncy ball. Typically, the heavier and smaller balls roll farther. Can you think of another size ball that we have that you can test?

Nature Study: Ramps in Nature

This week, you are looking for objects in natural ramps, or inclined planes. These could be found in rock formations, ant hills, drainage ditches, or the edges of a creek.

Preparation

↻ No preparation is needed for this week.

Outdoor Time

☼ Go on a walk with the students to look for inclined planes in nature. Take some time to roll a small rock or acorn down the inclined planes you find. Allow the students to make observations and discoveries about the inclined planes.

Coordinating Activities

✂ **Art** – (Ramp Painting) Give the student several marbles, a plate with some paint on it, a block of wood, and a piece of paper taped onto a thin sheet of cardboard to give it some strength. Have the student set up an inclined plane of paper using the block of wood. Next, roll the marbles in the paint, and then roll the marbles down the inclined plane. You could have the student vary the height of the ramp to change the speed of the marble, which will change the type of paint track it leaves behind.

✂ Snack – (Marshmallow Ramps) Give the students several whole graham crackers and a few marshmallows. Have them make an inclined plane out of the graham crackers and test it with their marshmallows. When they are done experimenting, let them eat their creations.

✂ Activity – (Water Droplet Race) You will need the ramp from the demonstration, a small bowl full of water, an eye dropper, and wax paper. Have them drop several drops of water at the top of the wax paper and see which one reaches the bottom first!

Write – Simple Notebooking

Student Diary

- ☐ Main Idea Page – Have the students color the coloring page found on SD p. 47.

- ☐ Demonstration Sheet – After you do the demonstration, fill out the demonstration sheet found on SD p. 48 with the students.

- ☐ Nature Journal Sheet – After you have your nature study time, fill out the nature journal sheet found on SD p. 49 with the students. The students can sketch what they have seen, or you can write down their observations.

- ☐ Art Page – Have the students use SD p. 50 to complete the art activity.

Lapbooking Templates

- 🗁 Weekly Mini-book – Have the students cut out and color the Inclined Planes Mini-book on LT p. 22. You can have them cut out the main idea graphic included and glue it in the interior of the mini-book, or you can write a sentence with what they have learned from the week for them on the inside of the mini-book. Once the students are done, have them glue the booklet into the mini-lapbook.

- 🗁 Overall Lapbook – Have them add the art project they did to the "My Physics Projects" pocket.

Week 5: Sound

2-Days-a-Week Schedule		
	Day 1	**Day 2**
Read	❑ Read the introduction with the students ❑ Read the selected pages in *The Usborne Children's Encyclopedia*	❑ Choose one or more of the additional books to read from this week
Do	❑ Complete the Scientific Demonstration "Tonoscope" ❑ Eat "Krispie Sounds" for snack	❑ Complete the Nature Study "Bird Calls" ❑ Do the "Plate Shakers" activity
Write	❑ Color the main idea page ❑ Fill out the demonstration sheet	❑ Fill out the nature journal sheet ❑ Complete the art page

5-Days-a-Week Schedule					
	Day 1	**Day 2**	**Day 3**	**Day 4**	**Day 5**
Read	❑ Read the introduction with the students	❑ Read the selected pages in *The Usborne Children's Encyclopedia*	❑ Choose one or more of the additional books to read from this week	❑ Choose one or more of the additional books to read from this week	
Do	❑ Eat "Krispie Sounds" for snack	❑ Complete the Scientific Demonstration "Tonoscope"	❑ Work on the activity "Marco Polo"	❑ Do the "Plate Shakers" activity	❑ Complete the Nature Study "Bird Calls"
Write	❑ Color the main idea page	❑ Fill out the demonstration sheet	❑ Complete the Sound Mini-book	❑ Complete the art page	❑ Fill out the nature journal sheet

Read – Information Gathering

Weekly Topic

🎵 Sound waves are vibrations that can travel through the air.

Scripted Introduction

Say to the students:

Fa-la-la-la-la, fa-la-la-la. Singing is sound.

? What do you know about sound?

Allow the student to share their ideas. Then, say to the students:

When I talk to you, you are hearing sound waves that leave my throat and travel through the air. Your ears receive it, and your brain unscrambles the information and let's you know what you are hearing.

This week, we are going to spend some time learning about sound.

Read–Alouds

Encyclopedia Pages

📖 *The Usborne Children's Encyclopedia* pp. 208-209 "Sound"

Library Books to Look For

📖 *Sound Waves (Energy in Action)* by Ian F. Mahaney
📖 *Oscar and the Bat: A Book About Sound (Start with Science)* by Geoff Waring
📖 *Sounds All Around (Let's-Read-and-Find... Science 1)* by Wendy Pfeffer and Holly Keller
📖 *All about Sound (Rookie Read-About Science)* by Lisa Trumbauer

Do – Hands-on Projects

Scientific Demonstration: Tonoscope

Materials Needed

✓ An empty yogurt container
✓ Wax paper
✓ Rubber band
✓ Salt
✓ Sound makers (such as a radio, metal pot lid, a wooden spoon, etc.)

Steps to Complete

1. Read the following introduction to your students:

   Remember earlier we heard in the introduction? Now, we are going to build a device that will allow us to see sound!

2. Begin by placing the wax paper over the top of the empty yogurt container, and use the rubber band to secure it in place. (Note—*You want the wax paper to cover the entire opening. It should be snug and taut, but not so tight that it causes distortion of the plastic container.*)

3. Set the covered container on a flat surface, and have the students gently add about a teaspoon of salt to the wax paper. Shake the container a bit so that the salt lies in one smooth layer that covers the top.

4. Next, have the students make noise near the tonoscope using a radio or by banging a metal pot lid with a wooden spoon. Ask the students:

   ? What happens to the salt?

Explanation

Read the following explaination to the students:

We saw the salt bounced and moved when sound was made near it. This is because the sound waves produced caused the solid salt particles to vibrate as the waves moved through.

Nature Study: Bird Calls

This week, you are studying sound. There are lots of sounds in nature, but the call of a bird is one of the easier ones to notice. Bird calls will be the focus of your nature study this week.

Preparation

↪ Read pp. 27-142 in the *Handbook of Nature Study* to learn more about birds. (Note—*Choose one or two birds that can be found in your area.*)

Outdoor Time

⚙ Go on a walk with the students to listen for birds. Allow the students to make observations about the sounds they here. You can use an app like Merlin Bird ID or SmartBird to help you identify the bird calls you hear. You can also use the information you have learned from reading the *Handbook of Nature Study* to answer their questions or to share information about any local birds they are observing.

Coordinating Activities

✂ **Art** – (Plate Shakers) Have the students make a sound producer using two paper plates, paint, tape, and beans. Have your student decorate the bottom of two paper plates by painting the picture of their choice. Then, put several beans on one of the plates. Flip the other plate over and place it on top. Use the tape to secure the two plates together. Finally, let the students shake and enjoy!

✂ **Snack** – (Krispie Sounds) Have the students observe the sound Rice Krispies can make. You will need Rice Krispies cereal, a bowl, milk, and a toilet paper tube. Pour a bowl of Rice Krispies and milk for the students. Have them listen to the bowl. Then, have them place the toilet paper tube up to their ear and place the other end near the bowl of cereal. Can they hear the cereal better now? Once they are done listening, have them eat and enjoy the cereal.

✂ **Activity** – (Marco Polo) Have the students play Marco Polo, which is a game that uses sound. Head outside or to a safe place for the students to play the game with eyes closed. The person who is it closes their eyes and yells out, "Marco." The rest of the players respond with "Polo," and the person who is it tries to find them. When they tag another person, that person becomes it, and the game begins again.

Write – Simple Notebooking

Student Diary

- ☐ **Main Idea Page** – Have the students color the coloring page found on SD p. 51.
- ☐ **Demonstration Sheet** – After you do the demonstration, fill out the demonstration sheet found on SD p. 52 with the students.
- ☐ **Nature Journal Sheet** – After you have your nature study time, fill out the nature journal sheet found on SD p. 53 with the students. The students can sketch what they have seen, or you can write down their observations.
- ☐ **Art Page** – Have the students take a picture of their plate shaker and glue it onto SD p. 54.

Lapbooking Templates

- 📁 **Weekly Mini-book** – Have the students cut out and color the Sound Mini-book on LT p. 23. You can have them cut out the main idea graphic included and glue it in the interior of the mini-book, or you can write a sentence with what they have learned from the week for them on the inside of the mini-book. Once the students are done, have them glue the booklet into the mini-lapbook.
- 📁 **Overall Lapbook** – Have them add a picture of the project they did to the "My Physics Projects" pocket.

Week 6: Light

2–Days–a–Week Schedule		
	Day 1	**Day 2**
Read	❑ Read the introduction with the students ❑ Read the selected pages in *The Usborne Children's Encyclopedia*	❑ Choose one or more of the additional books to read from this week
Do	❑ Complete the Scientific Demonstration "Shining Rainbows" ❑ Play the game "Flashlight Tag"	❑ Complete the Nature Study "The Sun" ❑ Do the "Reflection Collage" activity
Write	❑ Color the main idea page ❑ Fill out the demonstration sheet	❑ Fill out the nature journal sheet ❑ Complete the art page

5–Days–a–Week Schedule					
	Day 1	**Day 2**	**Day 3**	**Day 4**	**Day 5**
Read	❑ Read the introduction with the students	❑ Read the selected pages in *The Usborne Children's Encyclopedia*	❑ Choose one or more of the additional books to read from this week	❑ Choose one or more of the additional books to read from this week	
Do		❑ Complete the Scientific Demonstration "Shining Rainbows"	❑ Work on the activity "Flashlight Tag"	❑ Do the "Reflection Collage" activity	❑ Complete the Nature Study "The Sun"
Write	❑ Color the main idea page	❑ Fill out the demonstration sheet	❑ Complete the Light Mini-book	❑ Complete the art page	❑ Fill out the nature journal sheet

Read – Information Gathering

Weekly Topic

↳ Light is the type of energy that helps us to see.

Scripted Introduction

If possible, share this introduction while you are in a room with no windows. Start with the lights on. Say to the students:

> When the lights are on in a room, we can see a lot of things.
>
> **?** What do you see in this room?

Let the students look around and take time to answer your question. Then, say:

> Those are good observations. But if the lights aren't on, it is much harder for us to see the objects in the room.

(Note—*If the students are afraid of the dark, skip the next question.*)

If the students are not afraid of the dark, turn off the lights and ask the following question:

> **?** What do you see now?

Let the students look around and take time to answer your question. Then, turn back on the lights and say:

> It is a lot harder for us to see the things in the room when the lights are out. This is because light helps us to see. Light is actually a type of energy that helps us see.
>
> This week, we are going to look closer at light.

Read–Alouds

Encyclopedia Pages

📖 *The Usborne Children's Encyclopedia* pp. 206-207 "Light and Color" OR *The Usborne Children's Encyclopedia* pp. 192-193 "Energy"

Library Books to Look For

📖 *All About Light* (Rookie Read-About Science) by Lisa Trumbauer
📖 *Exploring Light* (How Does Science Work?) by Carol Ballard
📖 *The Magic School Bus: Gets A Bright Idea, The: A Book About Light* by Nancy White

Do – Hands-on Projects

Scientific Demonstration: Shining Rainbows

Materials Needed

- ✓ Bubble solution and wand

  Note—You can make your own bubble solution by following the directions found here:

  - ⌁ https://artfulparent.com/how-to-make-homemade-bubbles/

- ✓ Plate

Steps to Complete

1. Read the following introduction to your students:

   Remember earlier we saw how we need light to see? Well, sometimes that light is bent in different ways so that we see different colors. This is exactly what we are going to try to capture right now!

2. Have the students gently blow a few bubbles on the plate.

3. Then, have them observe the colors as light hits the bubbles. Ask them:

   ? What do you notice about the surface of the bubbles?

Explanation

Read the following explaination to the students:

We saw the colors of the rainbow seem to shimmer over the surface of the bubbles. This is because the light rays are reflected in different ways off the surface of the bubble. This effect causes the light rays to travel in different directions and allows our eyes to see the light as different colors.

Nature Study: The Sun

This week, you are going to look at the sun, our source of natural light during the day. (Note— *You will look at the sun again in the first week of the Meteorology unit.*)

Preparation

⌁ Read pp. 833-834 in the *Handbook of Nature Study* to learn more about the sun.

Outdoor Time

⌁ Go on a walk with the students to feel the power of the sun. Allow the students to observe the difference between being in the sun and being in the shade. You can use the information you have learned from reading the *Handbook of Nature Study* to answer their questions or to share information about what they are observing.

Coordinating Activities

✂ Art – (Reflection Collage) Go on a hunt for reflective materials in your house, or provide the students with a collection of reflective materials they can use to make their collage. Have them glue the materials on a sheet of paper, and then take it outside to see how the collage reflects the light.

✂ Activity – (Flashlight Tag) This game is best played at night or in a darkened room. For flashlight tag, you will use the same rules you would for a game a tag, except the person must be "touched" by a beam of light before they are "it." The person who is "it" has the flashlight.

Write – Simple Notebooking

Student Diary

☐ Main Idea Page – Have the students color the coloring page found on SD p. 55.

☐ Demonstration Sheet – After you do the demonstration, fill out the demonstration sheet found on SD p. 56 with the students.

☐ Nature Journal Sheet – After you have your nature study time, fill out the nature journal sheet found on SD p. 57 with the students. The students can sketch what they have seen, or you can write down their observations.

☐ Art Page – Have the students use SD p. 58 to complete the art activity.

Lapbooking Templates

📁 Weekly Mini-book – Have the students cut out and color the Light Mini-book on LT p. 24. You can have them cut out the main idea graphic included and glue it in the interior of the mini-book, or you can write a sentence with what they have learned from the week for them on the inside of the mini-book. Once the students are done, have them glue the booklet into the mini-lapbook.

📁 Overall Lapbook – Have them add the art project they did to the "My Physics Projects" pocket.

Intro to Science

Unit 3: Intro to Geology

Intro to Geology Unit Overview

Sequence for Study

- 🌏 Week 1: Fossils
- 🌏 Week 2: Rocks
- 🌏 Week 3: Metamorphic Rock
- 🌏 Week 4: Volcanoes
- 🌏 Week 5: Sedimentary Rock
- 🌏 Week 6: Compass

Supplies Needed for the Unit

Week	Introduction Props	Hands-on Project Materials	Coordinating Activities Supplies
1	Several pictures of fossils (or an actual fossil)	Air dry clay, Rubber insects or shells, Rolling pin	Sugar cookie dough, Several plant or animal stamps or stencils, Gray or brown paint, Paper
2	Several rocks from your area	Rock, Hammer	Rock candy, Several rocks you have collected, Several colors of paint, Medium sized rock
3	Several metamorphic rocks	Six different colors of crayon, Old grater, Aluminum foil, Bowl, Hot water	Peanut butter (or other nut butter), jelly, bread, Crayons, Paper, Cardboard, Hair dryer, Several rocks
4	*No supplies needed.*	Scissors or a knife, Tube of a toothpaste, Empty plastic yogurt container, Dirt	Paint (black, gray, orange, red), Paper, Paper cup, Crackers (saltines or Ritz™), Can of CheeseWhiz™
5	Sandstone	Glass or plastic jar with a lid, Sand, Gravel, Pebbles or small rocks, Water	Graham crackers Peanut butter, Sugar, Mini chocolate chips, Sand, Glue, Pebbles, Bread loaf pan, Plastic wrap, Paint, Sand, Paper
6	Compass, Map	Compass, Small treasure or candy, Paper, Pen	Sugar cookies, Icing, Pencil, Paper, Pin, Milk jug, Knife, Magnet

Books Scheduled

Hands-on Projects

- *Handbook of Nature Study (If you are using the nature study option.)*

Scheduled Encylopedias

- *The Usborne Children's Encyclopedia*

Library Books to Look For

Week 1

- *Mary Anning: Fossil Hunter* by Sally M. Walker and Phyllis V. Saroff
- *Viewfinder: Fossils* by Douglas Palmer and Neil D. L. Clark
- *What Do You Know About Fossils?* (20 Questions: Science) by Suzanne Slade
- *Fossils Tell of Long Ago* (Let's-Read-and-Find Out Science 2) by Aliki

Week 2

- *Looking at Rocks* (My First Field Guides) by Jennifer Dussling and Tim Haggerty
- *Rocks: Hard, Soft, Smooth, and Rough* (Amazing Science) by Rosinsky, Natalie M, John, and Matthew
- *Rocks and Fossils* (Science Kids) by Chris Pellant
- *Rocks! Rocks! Rocks!* by Nancy Elizabeth Wallace

Week 3

- *Metamorphic Rocks* (Earth Rocks!) by Holly Cefrey
- *I Love Rocks* (Rookie Readers, Level B) by Cari Meister and Terry Sirrell

Week 4

- *National Geographic Readers: Volcanoes!* by Anne Schreiber
- *Jump into Science: Volcano!* by Ellen J. Prager and Nancy Woodman
- *Volcanoes* (Let's-Read-and-Find... Science 2) by Franklyn M. Branley and Megan Lloyd
- *The Magic School Bus Blows Its Top: A Book About Volcanoes* (Magic School Bus) by Gail Herman and Bob Ostrom

Week 5

- *Sedimentary Rocks* (Earth Rocks!) by Holly Cefrey
- *Earthsteps: A Rock's Journey through Time* by Diane Nelson Spickert and Marianne D. Wallace

Week 6

- *You Can Use a Compass* (Rookie Read-About Science) by Lisa Trumbauer
- *North, South, East, and West* (Rookie Read-About Science) by Allan Fowler
- *Maps and Globes* by Jack Knowlton and Harriet Barton

Week 1: Fossils

You do not need to complete all of this in a week. Instead, choose from the following options.

2-Days-a-Week Schedule	Day 1	Day 2
Read	❑ Read the introduction with the students ❑ Read the selected pages in *The Usborne Children's Encyclopedia*	❑ Choose one or more of the additional books to read from this week
Do	❑ Complete the Scientific Demonstration "Impression Fossils" ❑ Eat "Fossil Cookies" for snack	❑ Complete the Nature Study "Fossil Find" ❑ Do the "Fossil Prints" activity
Write	❑ Color the main idea page ❑ Fill out the demonstration sheet	❑ Fill out the nature journal sheet ❑ Complete the art page

5-Days-a-Week Schedule	Day 1	Day 2	Day 3	Day 4	Day 5
Read	❑ Read the introduction with the students	❑ Read the selected pages in *The Usborne Children's Encyclopedia*	❑ Choose one or more of the additional books to read from this week	❑ Choose one or more of the additional books to read from this week	
Do	❑ Eat "Fossil Cookies" for snack	❑ Complete the Scientific Demonstration "Impression Fossils"	❑ Work on the activity "Dig 'Em Up"	❑ Do the "Fossil Prints" activity	❑ Complete the Nature Study "Fossil Find"
Write	❑ Color the main idea page	❑ Fill out the demonstration sheet	❑ Complete the Fossils Mini-book	❑ Complete the art page	❑ Fill out the nature journal sheet

Read – Information Gathering

Weekly Topic

- Fossils are imprints of long-gone plants or animals.

Scripted Introduction

Have several pictures of fossils from books and magazines (or have several rocks with fossils) on the table in front of you. As you show the pictures to the students, say:

This is a fossil. We find fossils in rocks all over the Earth.

They are the remains of plants or animals that died many years ago. When they died, they got stuck in the mud, and as time went by, more mud pressed on top of them.

Eventually, there was so much weight that the mud turned into rock, and the impression of the plant or animal was stuck in it.

? Can you find the plant or animal impression in these fossil pictures?

Give them time to observe the pictures (or fossils) before you say:

This week, we are going to look closer at fossils.

Read–Alouds

Encyclopedia Pages

- *The Usborne Children's Encyclopedia* p. 19 "Fossils"

Library Books to Look For

- *Mary Anning: Fossil Hunter* by Sally M. Walker and Phyllis V. Saroff
- *Viewfinder: Fossils* by Douglas Palmer and Neil D. L. Clark
- *What Do You Know About Fossils?* (20 Questions: Science) by Suzanne Slade
- *Fossils Tell of Long Ago* (Let's-Read-and-Find Out Science 2) by Aliki

Do – Hands-on Projects

Scientific Demonstration: Impression Fossils

Materials Needed

- ✓ Air dry clay
- ✓ Rubber insects or shells
- ✓ Rolling pin

Steps to Complete

1. Read the following introduction to your students:

    Remember earlier we saw the pictures of fossils? And how we learned that a fossil captures a plant or animal from long ago. Now, we are going to make our own fossil impression!

2. Have the students roll out the clay into a flat disc.

3. Then, have them place the rubber insects or shells in various places in the clay. Have them gently press the objects into the clay before picking them up. Ask the students:

    ? What do you see when you take the object away?

    (Note—You can set aside the clay model to let it dry overnight and have the students paint it the next day.)

Explanation

Read the following explaination to the students:

    We saw that the rubber insects or shells left an impression in our clay rock. This process is a shortened look at how impression fossils are made. We did it in an afternoon, but normally it takes much, much longer than that!

Nature Study: Fossil Find

This week, you are looking for fossils in nature. Although there are places that are easier to find fossils, fossils can be found anywhere. If fossils are not easy to find in your area, have one on hand to observe.

Preparation

📖 Read pp. 756-757 in the *Handbook of Nature Study* to learn more about fossils.

Outdoor Time

☼ Go on a walk with the students to look for fossils. Allow the students to make observations about any fossils they find. You can use the information you have learned from reading the *Handbook of Nature Study* to answer their questions or to share information about what they are observing.

Coordinating Activities

✂ Art – (Fossil Prints) Beforehand, collect several stamps or stencils that have a leaf, starfish, or other small plant or animal on it. Begin by having the students paint gray or brown paint on a sheet of paper. Then, have the students use the stamps or stencils with black paint to make fossils in their rocks.

✂ Snack – (Fossil Cookies) Make your favorite sugar cookie dough recipe. Have the students make rocks out of the cookies and then, using forks, spoon, knives, or fingers, create fossils on the cookies.

✂ Activity – (Dig 'Em Up Matching Game) Play a fossil matching game with your students. You can download the game through the following website:

🖰 https://www.partythroughtheusa.com/2019/01/fossil-dig-travel-matching-game. html

Write – Simple Notebooking

Student Diary

☐ Main Idea Page – Have the students color the coloring page found on SD p. 61.

☐ Demonstration Sheet – After you do the demonstration, fill out the demonstration sheet found on SD p. 62 with the students.

☐ Nature Journal Sheet – After you have your nature study time, fill out the nature journal sheet found on SD p. 63 with the students. The students can sketch what they have seen, or you can write down their observations.

☐ Art Page – Have the students use SD p. 64 to complete the art activity.

Lapbooking Templates

📁 Weekly Mini-book – Have the students cut out and color the Fossils Mini-book on LT p. 29. You can have them cut out the main idea graphic included and glue it in the interior of the mini-book, or you can write a sentence with what they have learned from the week for them on the inside of the mini-book. Once the students are done, have them glue the booklet into the mini-lapbook.

📁 Overall Lapbook – Have the students cut out the "My Geology Projects" pocket on LT p. 35. Have them glue the pocket into the lapbook and add the coloring project they did to the pocket.

Week 2: Rocks

2-Days-a-Week Schedule		
	Day 1	**Day 2**
Read	❑ Read the introduction with the students ❑ Read the selected pages in *The Usborne Children's Encyclopedia*	❑ Choose one or more of the additional books to read from this week
Do	❑ Complete the Scientific Demonstration "Rocky Observations" ❑ Eat "Rock Candy" for snack	❑ Complete the Nature Study "Rock Hunt" ❑ Do the "Painting Rocks" activity
Write	❑ Color the main idea page ❑ Fill out the demonstration sheet	❑ Fill out the nature journal sheet ❑ Complete the art page

5-Days-a-Week Schedule					
	Day 1	**Day 2**	**Day 3**	**Day 4**	**Day 5**
Read	❑ Read the introduction with the students	❑ Read the selected pages in *The Usborne Children's Encyclopedia*	❑ Choose one or more of the additional books to read from this week	❑ Choose one or more of the additional books to read from this week	
Do	❑ Eat "Rock Candy" for snack	❑ Complete the Scientific Demonstration "Rocky Observations"	❑ Work on the activity "Classifying Rocks"	❑ Do the "Painting Rocks" activity	❑ Complete the Nature Study "Rock Hunt"
Write	❑ Color the main idea page	❑ Fill out the demonstration sheet	❑ Complete the Rocks Mini-book	❑ Complete the art page	❑ Fill out the nature journal sheet

Read – Information Gathering

Weekly Topic

⤷ There are many different types of rocks.

Scripted Introduction

Have several rocks from your area on the table in front of you. Say to the students:

> There are many different types of rocks, and they have many different uses. Rocks are used to build buildings, to form statues, and to create clay pots.

> We can find rocks almost anywhere. These are several of the types of rocks you can find where we live.

> **?** What do you notice about these rocks?

Give them time to observe the rocks before you say:

> This week, we are going to spend some time collecting and looking at rocks.

If you have a rock field guide on hand, give the students some time to look through the guide.

Read-Alouds

Encyclopedia Pages

📖 *The Usborne Children's Encyclopedia* p. 18 "Rocks"

Library Books to Look For

📖 *Looking at Rocks* (My First Field Guides) by Jennifer Dussling and Tim Haggerty
📖 *Rocks: Hard, Soft, Smooth, and Rough* (Amazing Science) by Rosinsky, Natalie M, John, and Matthew
📖 *Rocks and Fossils* (Science Kids) by Chris Pellant
📖 *Rocks! Rocks! Rocks!* by Nancy Elizabeth Wallace

Do – Hands-on Projects

Scientific Demonstration: Rocky Observation

Materials Needed

✓ Rock
✓ Hammer

Steps to Complete

1. Read the following introduction to your students:

Remember earlier we saw several different types of rocks and learned how they can be used? Now, we are going to look at one rock up close, so we can make some scientific observations!

2. Have the students make observe the rock. As they observe, ask them:

   ? How does the rock smell?

   ? How does the rock feel?

   ? What do you see on the surface of the rock?

   ? What color is the rock?

3. Have the students watch as you hit the rock with a hammer

   ? What happens when I hit it with a hammer?

   ? What happens when you use the rock to mark on a paper?

Explanation

The results will vary depending on the rock you observe, so there is no explanation to read for this demonstration.

Nature Study: Rock Hunt

This week, you are looking for rocks in nature.

Preparation

⟳ Read pp. 743-745 in the *Handbook of Nature Study* to learn more about rocks.

Outdoor Time

☼ Go on a walk with the students to look for rocks. Allow the students to make observations about any rocks they find. You can use the information you have learned from reading the *Handbook of Nature Study* to answer their questions or to share information about what they are observing.

Coordinating Activities

✂ **Art** – (Painting Rocks) Give the students several colors of paint and a medium-sized rock that they have collected. Let them choose the design they want to paint on the rock.

✂ **Snack** – (Rock Candy) Get some rock candy to eat for snack, or make your own using the recipe in the appendix p. 191.

✂ **Activity** – (Classifying Rocks) Using a rock field guide or the Internet, classify the rocks the students collected during the nature study. You will need to heavily guide the students through this activity.

Write – Simple Notebooking

Student Diary

- ☐ **Main Idea Page** – Have the students color the coloring page found on SD p. 65.
- ☐ **Demonstration Sheet** – After you do the demonstration, fill out the demonstration sheet found on SD p. 66 with the students.
- ☐ **Nature Journal Sheet** – After you have your nature study time, fill out the nature journal sheet found on SD p. 67 with the students. The students can sketch what they have seen, or you can write down their observations.
- ☐ **Art Page** – Have the students take a picture or their rock and have the students glue a picture of their painted rock on SD p. 68 to complete the art activity.

Lapbooking Templates

- 📁 **Weekly Mini-book** – Have the students cut out and color the Rocks Mini-book on LT p. 30. You can have them cut out the main idea graphic included and glue it in the interior of the mini-book, or you can write a sentence with what they have learned from the week for them on the inside of the mini-book. Once the students are done, have them glue the booklet into the mini-lapbook.
- 📁 **Overall Lapbook** – Have the students add the page they painted to the "My Geology Projects" pocket in the lapbook.

Week 3: Metamorphic Rock

2–Days–a–Week Schedule		
	Day 1	**Day 2**
Read	❑ Read the introduction with the students ❑ Read the selected pages in *The Usborne Children's Encyclopedia*	❑ Choose one or more of the additional books to read from this week
Do	❑ Complete the Scientific Demonstration "Changed Rocks" ❑ Eat "Metamorphic Rock Sandwich" for snack	❑ Complete the Nature Study "Metamorphic Rock Hunt" ❑ Do the "Metamorphic Art" activity
Write	❑ Color the main idea page ❑ Fill out the demonstration sheet	❑ Fill out the nature journal sheet ❑ Complete the art page

5–Days–a–Week Schedule					
	Day 1	**Day 2**	**Day 3**	**Day 4**	**Day 5**
Read	❑ Read the introduction with the students	❑ Read the selected pages in *The Usborne Children's Encyclopedia*	❑ Choose one or more of the additional books to read from this week	❑ Choose one or more of the additional books to read from this week	
Do	❑ Eat "Metamorphic Rock Sandwich" for snack	❑ Complete the Scientific Demonstration "Changed Rocks"	❑ Work on the activity "Rock Band"	❑ Do the "Metamorphic Art" activity	❑ Complete the Nature Study "Metamorphic Rock Hunt"
Write	❑ Color the main idea page	❑ Fill out the demonstration sheet	❑ Complete the Metamorphic Rock Mini-book	❑ Complete the art page	❑ Fill out the nature journal sheet

Read – Information Gathering

Weekly Topic

↳ Metamorphic rocks are rocks that have changed.

Scripted Introduction

Have several metamorphic rocks (marble, granite, limestone, or slate are good examples) on the table in front of you. Say to the students:

> Metamorphic rocks are a special type of rock that has been changed by heat and pressure. These rocks start out as layers of dead organic material or bits of other rocks, which are smushed into sedimentary rock. Then, over time, the sedimentary rock is pressed and smashed to form metamorphic rock. So, by the time a rock becomes metamorphic rock, it has undergone several changes.

Pick up one of the rocks from the table and ask:

> **?** What do you notice about this rock?

Give them time to observe all of the rocks before you say:

> This week, we are going to look closer at different types of metamorphic rock.

Read–Alouds

Encyclopedia Pages

📖 *The Usborne Children's Encyclopedia* – There are no new pages scheduled.

Library Books to Look For

📖 *Metamorphic Rocks* (Earth Rocks!) by Holly Cefrey
📖 *I Love Rocks* (Rookie Readers, Level B) by Cari Meister and Terry Sirrell

Do – Hands-on Projects

Scientific Demonstration: Changed Rocks

Materials Needed
- ✓ Six different colors of crayon
- ✓ Old grater
- ✓ Aluminum foil
- ✓ Bowl
- ✓ Hot water

Steps to Complete

1. Read the following introduction to your students:

Remember earlier we observed a metamorphic rock? This type of rock changes over time. Now, we are going to use crayons to create our own changed rocks!

2. Have the students unwrap the crayons and shape the piece of aluminum foil into a mini-bowl that will just fit inside of the bowl.

3. Then, have the students grate half of each crayon into the piece of aluminum foil.

4. {**Adults Only**} Pour the hot water into the bowl.

5. Meanwhile, have the students twist the edges of the aluminum foil up to form a closed packet. Then, have the students gently set the packet into the water. Let the bowl sit undisturbed for one to two minutes or until the contents are soft.

6. {**Adults Only**} Remove the foil packet.

7. Once the packet is cool enough to touch, have the students use their hands to squeeze the packet into a crayon rock.

8. Open up the foil packet. Ask the students:

   ? What happened to the crayons?

Explanation

Read the following explaination to the students:

> When we opened the foil, we saw a rock ball with swirls. We also saw that some of the colors have mixed. The crayon rock ball we created is similar to a piece of metamorphic rock because it was changed by heat and pressure.

Nature Study: Metamorphic Rock Hunt

This week, you are looking for metamorphic rocks in nature. If metamorphic rocks are not easy to find in your area, have a piece on hand to observe.

Preparation

↻ Read pp. 748-749 in the *Handbook of Nature Study* to learn more about metamorphic rock.

Outdoor Time

Go on a walk with the students to look for calcite, granite, slate, limestone, or marble. Allow the students to make observations about what they find. You can use the information you have learned from reading the *Handbook of Nature Study* to answer their questions or to share information about what they are observing.

Coordinating Activities

✂ **Art** – (Metamorphic Art) Let the students choose three to five crayons that they love and hand them to you. Set a sheet of paper on a piece of cardboard, and set the crayons at the end of a sheet of paper. Using a hair dryer, gently apply heat to the crayons so that the wax melts and spreads on the sheet of paper. Let the designs completely cool before you let the students touch the designs.

✂ Snack – (Metamorphic Rock Sandwich) Make a peanut butter and jelly sandwich using chunky peanut butter. (Note—*If the students are allergic to peanuts, use another nut butter with a few chopped seeds or nuts sprinkled on top.*) Cut it in half and set one half of the sandwich aside. (*This is your sedimentary rock sandwich-rock formed layer by layer.*) Then take the other half and apply pressure. (*This is your metamorphic rock sandwich-rock that is formed when the layers of sedimentary rock are put under pressure.*) Taste both sandwiches and talk about the differences between them.

✂ Activity – (Rock Band) Have the students use the rocks that were collected last week or this week to make a bit of music. You can have them tap different rocks together. You can have them tap the rocks on different surfaces. You can have them roll the rocks around a pie plate. Whatever you choose, have them students compare the sounds that the different rocks make.

Write – Simple Notebooking

Student Diary

☐ Main Idea Page – Have the students color the coloring page found on SD p. 69.

☐ Demonstration Sheet – After you do the demonstration, fill out the demonstration sheet found on SD p. 70 with the students.

☐ Nature Journal Sheet – After you have your nature study time, fill out the nature journal sheet found on SD p. 71 with the students. The students can sketch what they have seen, or you can write down their observations.

☐ Art Page – Have the students use SD p. 72 to complete the art activity.

Lapbooking Templates

📁 Weekly Mini-book – Have the students cut out and color the Metamorphic Rock Mini-book on LT p. 31. You can have them cut out the main idea graphic included and glue it in the interior of the mini-book, or you can write a sentence with what they have learned from the week for them on the inside of the mini-book. Once the students are done, have them glue the booklet into the mini-lapbook.

📁 Overall Lapbook – Have the students add the page they painted to the "My Geology Projects" pocket in the lapbook.

Week 4: Volcano

2-Days-a-Week Schedule		
	Day 1	**Day 2**
Read	❑ Read the introduction with the students ❑ Read the selected pages in *The Usborne Children's Encyclopedia*	❑ Choose one or more of the additional books to read from this week
Do	❑ Complete the Scientific Demonstration "Toothpaste Volcano" ❑ Eat "Cheese-cano" for snack	❑ Complete the Nature Study "Igneous Rock" ❑ Do the "My Volcano" activity
Write	❑ Color the main idea page ❑ Fill out the demonstration sheet	❑ Fill out the nature journal sheet ❑ Complete the art page

5-Days-a-Week Schedule					
	Day 1	**Day 2**	**Day 3**	**Day 4**	**Day 5**
Read	❑ Read the introduction with the students	❑ Read the selected pages in *The Usborne Children's Encyclopedia*	❑ Choose one or more of the additional books to read from this week	❑ Choose one or more of the additional books to read from this week	
Do	❑ Eat "Cheese-cano" for snack	❑ Complete the Scientific Demonstration "Toothpaste Volcano"	❑ Work on the activity "Volcano Video"	❑ Do the "My Volcano" activity	❑ Complete the Nature Study "Igneous Rock"
Write	❑ Color the main idea page	❑ Fill out the demonstration sheet	❑ Complete the Volcano Mini-book	❑ Complete the art page	❑ Fill out the nature journal sheet

Read – Information Gathering

Weekly Topic

- Volcanoes explode hot, sticky rock from inside the Earth.

Scripted Introduction

Say to the students:

Volcanoes are found all over the world, including under the sea.

The center of a volcano is filled with hot rock, called magma, which comes from deep inside the Earth. When the magma gets too hot, pressure builds up, and eventually the volcano blows its top!

When this happens, it spills out ash and hot, sticky rock, which we call lava. This week, we are going to make our own volcano and have a pretend explosion!

If you would like to show your students a bit more about Hawaii's volcanoes, we recommend watching the following video together:

🖰 https://www.youtube.com/watch?v=uhZTZShA1dc

Read–Alouds

Encyclopedia Pages

📖 *The Usborne Children's Encyclopedia* – There are no new pages scheduled.

Library Books to Look For

📖 *National Geographic Readers: Volcanoes!* by Anne Schreiber
📖 *Jump into Science: Volcano!* by Ellen J. Prager and Nancy Woodman
📖 *Volcanoes* (Let's-Read-and-Find... Science 2) by Franklyn M. Branley and Megan Lloyd
📖 *The Magic School Bus Blows Its Top: A Book About Volcanoes* (Magic School Bus) by Gail Herman and Bob Ostrom

Do – Hands-on Projects

Scientific Demonstration: Toothpaste Volcano

Materials Needed

- ✓ Scissors or a knife
- ✓ Tube of a toothpaste
- ✓ Empty plastic yogurt container

✓ Dirt

Steps to Complete

1. Read the following introduction to your students:

    Remember earlier we learned about volcanoes? Now, we are going to see how one erupts using toothpaste!

2. {**Adults Only**} Use a pair of scissors or a knife to cut a hole large enough to fit the tip of a toothpaste tube on the bottom of an empty plastic yogurt container. Remove the cap from a toothpaste tube, and insert it in the hole you just cut.

3. Have the students help you fill the yogurt container about two-thirds of the way full with dirt, and pack it down gently.

4. Then, have the students squeeze the toothpaste tube and see what happens! When they are done, ask them:

    ? What did you see?

Explanation

Read the following explaination to the students:

We saw the toothpaste "erupt" out of the dirt. It did take a bit of effort to make that happen, but that's exaclty like a real volcano. The pressure builds and builds, then it releases in an eruption.

Nature Study: Igneous Rock

This week, you are studying volcanoes. Igneous rocks are rocks formed by volcanoes, so they will be the focus of your nature study this week. If igneous rocks are not easy to find in your area, have a piece on hand to observe.

Preparation

📖 Read pp. 746-747 in the *Handbook of Nature Study* to learn more about igneous rock.

Outdoor Time

☼ Go on a walk with the students to look for igneous rocks. Allow the students to make observations about what they find. You can use the information you have learned from reading the *Handbook of Nature Study* to answer their questions or to share information about what they are observing.

Coordinating Activities

✂ Art – (My Volcano) Give the students some black, gray, orange, and red paint. Have them paint their own volcano on a sheet of paper. You can also add some texture to their volcano by adding salt or cornstarch to the paint.

✂ **Snack** – (Cheese-cano) Have the students make an edible volcano. You will need a paper cup, crackers (saltines or Ritz™), and a can of CheeseWhiz™. Poke a hole in the bottom of the paper cup just large enough to insert the tip of the CheeseWhiz™ can. Then, crush up the crackers so that you have some fine dust and some larger pieces. Add the crushed crackers to the cup to create a two- to three-inch thick layer of "dirt and rock." Now, push the tip of the CheeseWhiz™ can to let the "magma" flow. Observe what happens. (*Note— The students should see that the cheese pushes the crushed crackers out of the way and erupts at the top of the layer.*) Once your students are done observing, they can eat their volcanic creations.

✂ **Activity** – (Volcano Video) Have the students watch the following video about volcanoes:

🖰 https://www.youtube.com/watch?v=V863xR0Y2qk

Write – Simple Notebooking

Student Diary

- ☐ **Main Idea Page** – Have the students color the coloring page found on SD p. 73.
- ☐ **Demonstration Sheet** – After you do the demonstration, fill out the demonstration sheet found on SD p. 74 with the students.
- ☐ **Nature Journal Sheet** – After you have your nature study time, fill out the nature journal sheet found on SD p. 75 with the students. The students can sketch what they have seen, or you can write down their observations.
- ☐ **Art Page** – Have the students use SD p. 76 to complete the art activity.

Lapbooking Templates

- 📁 **Weekly Mini-book** – Have the students cut out and color the Volcanoes Mini-book on LT p. 32. You can have them cut out the main idea graphic included and glue it in the interior of the mini-book, or you can write a sentence with what they have learned from the week for them on the inside of the mini-book. Once the students are done, have them glue the booklet into the mini-lapbook.
- 📁 **Overall Lapbook** – Have the students add the page they painted to the "My Geology Projects" pocket in the lapbook.

Week 5: Sedimentary Rock

2-Days-a-Week Schedule		
	Day 1	**Day 2**
Read	❑ Read the introduction with the students ❑ Read the selected pages in *The Usborne Children's Encyclopedia*	❑ Choose one or more of the additional books to read from this week
Do	❑ Complete the Scientific Demonstration "Sediment Jar" ❑ Eat "Sedimentary Cookies" for snack	❑ Complete the Nature Study "Sedimentary Rock" ❑ Do the "Sand Painting" activity
Write	❑ Color the main idea page ❑ Fill out the demonstration sheet	❑ Fill out the nature journal sheet ❑ Complete the art page

5-Days-a-Week Schedule					
	Day 1	**Day 2**	**Day 3**	**Day 4**	**Day 5**
Read	❑ Read the introduction with the students	❑ Read the selected pages in *The Usborne Children's Encyclopedia*	❑ Choose one or more of the additional books to read from this week	❑ Choose one or more of the additional books to read from this week	
Do	❑ Eat "Sedimentary Cookies" for snack	❑ Complete the Scientific Demonstration "Sediment Jar"	❑ Work on the activity "Make Sandstone"	❑ Do the "Sand Painting" activity	❑ Complete the Nature Study "Sedimentary Rock"
Write	❑ Color the main idea page	❑ Fill out the demonstration sheet	❑ Complete the Sedimentary Rock Mini-book	❑ Complete the art page	❑ Fill out the nature journal sheet

Read – Information Gathering

Weekly Topic

- Sedimentary rock is made from layers of sand, mud, or pebbles.

Scripted Introduction

Have a piece of sandstone out on the table in front of you. Say to the students:

This is a piece of rock is called sandstone, which is a type of sedimentary rock. Sedimentary rock is formed layer by layer. As sand, mud, and pebbles settle, they build up and squeeze together to form rock.

? Can you see the layers in this rock?

? How about the bits of sand?

Give them time to observe all of the rocks before you say:

Those are good observations!

This piece of sandstone was formed from lots and lots of layers of sand that were pressed together over time. This week, we are going to look at sedimentary rocks.

Read–Alouds

Encyclopedia Pages

- *The Usborne Children's Encyclopedia* – There are no new pages scheduled.

Library Books to Look For

- *Sedimentary Rocks* (Earth Rocks!) by Holly Cefrey
- *Earthsteps: A Rock's Journey through Time* by Diane Nelson Spickert and Marianne D. Wallace

Do – Hands-on Projects

Scientific Demonstration: Sediment Jar

Materials Needed

- ✓ A glass or plastic jar with a lid
- ✓ A handful of sand
- ✓ A handful of gravel
- ✓ A handful of pebbles or small rocks
- ✓ Water

Steps to Complete

1. Read the following introduction to your students:

    Remember earlier we saw a piece of sandstone? We learned how this sediementary rock is formed. Now, we are going to see a small part of that process!

2. Set the jar on a flat surface, and have the students pour the sand into the bottom of the jar, followed by the gravel, and then pour in the small rocks.

3. Fill the jar almost to the top with water. Screw the lid on as tightly as you can (secure it with duct tape if your lid isn't tight).

4. Have the students shake the jar so that everything is mixed up well.

5. Then place the jar back on to the surface, and have them observe what happens as the layers settle. When things settle, ask the students:

    ? What happened to the rocks and sand after the jar sat for awhile?

Explanation

Read the following explaination to the students:

> We saw lighter sand and sediments forming on the top layer over the rocks. This is called the "fining up," and it is part of how sedimentary rocks form over time.

(Note—*You may also notice silt in the water, which will eventually settle.*)

Nature Study: Sedimentary Rock

This week, you are looking for sedimentary rocks in nature. If sedimentary rocks are not easy to find in your area, have a piece on hand to observe.

Preparation

✎ Read the p. 745 in the *Handbook of Nature Study* to learn more about sedimentary rock.

Outdoor Time

☼ Go on a walk with the students to look for sedimentary rocks. Allow the students to make observations about what they find. You can use the information you have learned from reading the *Handbook of Nature Study* to answer their questions or to share information about what they are observing.

Coordinating Activities

✂ Art – (Sand Painting) Give the students some paint in the color of their choice and a bowl with sand in it. Have them mix the paint and sand together, and then have the students use the sand paint to create a picture on a piece of paper.

✂ **Snack** – (Sedimentary Cookies) Use graham crackers as a base, peanut butter (or other nut butter) for the mud, sugar for the sand, and mini chocolate chips for the pebbles. Have your students layer their graham cracker with mud, sand, and pebbles and top it with another graham cracker. Then, squeeze the layers together gently, like sedimentary rock, eat, and enjoy.

✂ **Activity** – (Make Sandstone) Have the students mix together 2 cups of sand and ½ cup of glue. You can also add a few pebbles in as well. Press this mixture into a bread loaf pan that has been lined with plastic wrap. Cover with plastic wrap, and press as hard as you can to really squeeze the mixture together. Let it dry, and you will have your own sandstone.

Write – Simple Notebooking

Student Diary

☐ **Main Idea Page** – Have the students color the coloring page found on SD p. 77.

☐ **Demonstration Sheet** – After you do the demonstration, fill out the demonstration sheet found on SD p. 78 with the students.

☐ **Nature Journal Sheet** – After you have your nature study time, fill out the nature journal sheet found on SD p. 79 with the students. The students can sketch what they have seen, or you can write down their observations.

☐ **Art Page** – Have the students use SD p. 80 to complete the art activity.

Lapbooking Templates

📁 **Weekly Mini-book** – Have the students cut out and color the Sedimentary Rock Mini-book on LT p. 33. You can have them cut out the main idea graphic included and glue it in the interior of the mini-book, or you can write a sentence with what they have learned from the week for them on the inside of the mini-book. Once the students are done, have them glue the booklet into the mini-lapbook.

📁 **Overall Lapbook** – Have the students add the page they painted to the "My Geology Projects" pocket in the lapbook.

Week 6: Compass

2-Days-a-Week Schedule		
	Day 1	**Day 2**
Read	❑ Read the introduction with the students ❑ Read the selected pages in *The Usborne Children's Encyclopedia*	❑ Choose one or more of the additional books to read from this week
Do	❑ Complete the Scientific Demonstration "Treasure Hunt" ❑ Eat "Compass Cookies" for snack	❑ Complete the Nature Study "Nature Map" ❑ Do the "Room Map" activity
Write	❑ Color the main idea page ❑ Fill out the demonstration sheet	❑ Fill out the nature journal sheet ❑ Complete the art page

5-Days-a-Week Schedule					
	Day 1	**Day 2**	**Day 3**	**Day 4**	**Day 5**
Read	❑ Read the introduction with the students	❑ Read the selected pages in *The Usborne Children's Encyclopedia*	❑ Choose one or more of the additional books to read from this week	❑ Choose one or more of the additional books to read from this week	
Do	❑ Eat "Compass Cookies" for snack	❑ Complete the Scientific Demonstration "Treasure Hunt"	❑ Work on the activity "Homemade Compass"	❑ Do the "Room Map" activity	❑ Complete the Nature Study "Nature Map"
Write	❑ Color the main idea page	❑ Fill out the demonstration sheet	❑ Complete the Compass Mini-book	❑ Complete the art page	❑ Fill out the nature journal sheet

Read – Information Gathering

Weekly Topic

↳ A compass shows us north, south, east, and west.

Scripted Introduction

Have a compass and a map with a compass rose on it on the table in front of you. Say to the students:

> This is a compass. We use it to tell us which direction we are going or to find where north is.

Let the students hold the compass and observe how it works. Then say:

> Every map has a compass rose on it. The compass rose shows us where north, south, east, and west are on a map.

> This is so we can use a map of an area and a compass to guide you to where you want to go. This week, we are going to spend some more time learning about compasses and maps.

Read-Alouds

Encyclopedia Pages

📖 *The Usborne Children's Encyclopedia* – There are no new pages scheduled.

Library Books to Look For

📖 *You Can Use a Compass* (Rookie Read-About Science) by Lisa Trumbauer
📖 *North, South, East, and West* (Rookie Read-About Science) by Allan Fowler
📖 *Maps and Globes* by Jack Knowlton and Harriet Barton

Do – Hands-on Projects

Scientific Demonstration: Treasure Hunt

Materials Needed

✓ Compass
✓ Small treasure or candy
✓ Paper
✓ Pen

Steps to Complete

1. {**Adults Only**} Ahead of time hide the small treasure or candy. Then, draw a map using the

paper and pen for the students to follow. The directions should be something like, "Take 5 steps north. Then, take 3 steps east."

2. When everything is ready, read the following introduction to your students:

   Remember earlier we saw what a compass was and how to use it? Now, we are going to use that compas to find a treasure!

3. Have the students follow the map you created to find the treasure.

Explanation

There is no explanation for this demonstration because the point was to have the students use a compass in a fun way.

Nature Study: Nature Map

This week, your students will practice using a compass and a map in their backyard or in a park.

Preparation

✏ Make a map of a path through your backyard or a park, complete with natural landmarks and a compass rose. Write up directions using north, east, south, and west to give to the students so that they can use their compass to follow your map.

Outdoor Time

☼ Go on a walk outdoors with the students. Have them use your directions and map to guide the walk.

Coordinating Activities

✂ Art – (Room Map) Have the students choose a room in your house. Use a compass to find where north, south, east, and west are in the room. Next, have the students draw the compass rose on a sheet of paper. Then, have them create a map showing some items in the room.

✂ Snack – (Compass Cookies) Make your favorite sugar cookies, and then use icing to decorate them with the compass rose. Eat and enjoy.

✂ Activity – (Homemade Compass) Have the students make their own compass. You will need a straight pin, a milk jug, a knife, and a magnet. You can find the directions for this here:

   🖱 https://elementalscience.com/blogs/science-activities/how-to-make-a-compass

Write – Simple Notebooking

Student Diary

- ☐ **Main Idea Page** – Have the students color the coloring page found on SD p. 81.
- ☐ **Demonstration Sheet** – After you do the demonstration, fill out the demonstration sheet found on SD p. 82 with the students.
- ☐ **Nature Journal Sheet** – After you have your nature study time, fill out the nature journal sheet found on SD p. 83 with the students. The students should sketch a map of your walk complete with a compass rose and a few natural landmarks.
- ☐ **Art Page** – Have the students use SD p. 84 to complete the art activity.

Lapbooking Templates

- 📁 **Weekly Mini-book** – Have the students cut out and color the Compass Mini-book on LT p. 34. You can have them cut out the main idea graphic included and glue it in the interior of the mini-book, or you can write a sentence with what they have learned from the week for them on the inside of the mini-book. Once the students are done, have them glue the booklet into the mini-lapbook.
- 📁 **Overall Lapbook** – Have the students add the page they painted to the "My Geology Projects" pocket in the lapbook.

Intro to Science

Unit 4: Intro to Meteorology

Intro to Meteorology Unit Overview

Sequence for Study

- 🌞 Week 1: The Sun
- 🌞 Week 2: The Water Cycle
- 🌞 Week 3: The Seasons
- 🌞 Week 4: Wind
- 🌞 Week 5: Tornadoes
- 🌞 Week 6: Thermometer

Supplies Needed for the Unit

Week	Introduction Props	Hands-on Project Materials	Coordinating Activities Supplies
1	*No supplies needed.*	Muffin tin, Foil, Clear plastic wrap, Marshmallows, Chocolate chips, Butter	Orange, SunPrint paper, Several squares of red, yellow, and orange tissue paper, Paper
2	Water Cycle Picture from p. 188 of the Appendix	Clear glass jar, Jar lid or bowl, Ice cubes, Hot water	Egg whites, Cream of Tartar, Vanilla, Sugar, Small spray bottle or eyedropper, Blue paint, Paper
3	*No supplies needed.*	Weather Stickers (appendix p. 194)	Bananas, Grapes, Strawberries, Raisins, Carrots, Skewers, Paper, Seasonal pictures from magazines
4	*No supplies needed.*	Bubble mixture, Bubble wand	Blue Jell-O, Cool Whip, Container of bubbles, Paper, String, 2 Sticks
5	Pictures of tornadoes	Pint-sized Mason jar, Dish soap, Vinegar, Water, Glitter	Frozen fruit, Ice cream, Milk or juice, Thick paintbrush, Paper, Black and white paint, Plate, 2 Plastic bottles, Washer, Duct tape
6	Thermometer	2 Clear cups, Food coloring, Water (hot and ice-cold), Thermometer	Variety of hot and cold foods, Pictures of things to do or wear when it is hot or cold, Modeling clay, Food coloring, Water, Clear straw, Rubbing alcohol, Small bottle

Books Scheduled

Hands-on Projects

- *Handbook of Nature Study (If you are using the nature study option.)*

Scheduled Encylopedias

- *The Usborne Children's Encyclopedia*

Library Books to Look For

Week 1

- *The Sun: Our Nearest Star* (Let's-Read-and-Find Out) by Franklyn M. Branley and Edward Miller
- *Wake Up, Sun!* (Step-Into-Reading, Step 1) by David L. Harrison
- *The Sun Is My Favorite Star* by Frank Asch

Week 2

- *The Water Cycle* (First Facts, Water All Around) by Rebecca Olien
- *The Magic School Bus Wet All Over: A Book About The Water Cycle* by Pat Relf and Carolyn Bracken

Week 3

- *Watching the Seasons* (Welcome Books) by Edana Eckart
- *Sunshine Makes the Seasons* (Let's-Read-and-Find... Science 2) by Franklyn M. Branley and Michael Rex
- *Our Seasons* by Ranida T. Mckneally and Grace Lin

Week 4

- *Feel the Wind* (Let's-Read-and-Find... Science 2) by Arthur Dorros
- *The Wind Blew* by Pat Hutchins
- *Can You See the Wind?* (Rookie Read-About Science) by Allan Fowler

Week 5

- *Tornado Alert* (Let's-Read-and-Find... Science 2) by Franklyn M. Branley and Giulio Maestro
- *Tornadoes!* (DK READERS) by DK Publishing
- *The Terrifying Tub Tornado* by Ann K. Larson

Week 6

- *What Is a Thermometer* (Rookie Read-About Science) by Lisa Trumbauer
- *Thermometers* (First Facts. Science Tools) by Adele Richardson
- *Temperature* (Blastoff! Readers, First Science) by Kay Manolis
- *Too, Too Hot* (Reader's Clubhouse Level 1 Reader) by Judy Kentor Schmauss

Week 1: The Sun

You do not need to complete all of this in a week. Instead, choose from the following options.

2-Days-a-Week Schedule		
	Day 1	**Day 2**
Read	❏ Read the introduction with the students ❏ Read the selected pages in *The Usborne Children's Encyclopedia*	❏ Choose one or more of the additional books to read from this week
Do	❏ Complete the Scientific Demonstration "Solar Melt" ❏ Eat "Sun Slices" for snack	❏ Complete the Nature Study "Sunny Observations" ❏ Do the "Tissue Paper Sun" activity
Write	❏ Color the main idea page ❏ Fill out the demonstration sheet	❏ Fill out the nature journal sheet ❏ Complete the art page

5-Days-a-Week Schedule					
	Day 1	**Day 2**	**Day 3**	**Day 4**	**Day 5**
Read	❏ Read the introduction with the students	❏ Read the selected pages in *The Usborne Children's Encyclopedia*	❏ Choose one or more of the additional books to read from this week	❏ Choose one or more of the additional books to read from this week	
Do	❏ Eat "Sun Slices" for snack	❏ Complete the Scientific Demonstration "Solar Melt"	❏ Work on the activity "Sun Pictures"	❏ Do the "Tissue Paper Sun" activity	❏ Complete the Nature Study "Sunny Observations"
Write	❏ Color the main idea page	❏ Fill out the demonstration sheet	❏ Complete the Sun Mini-book	❏ Complete the art page	❏ Fill out the nature journal sheet

Read – Information Gathering

Weekly Topic

- The energy from the sun heats our Earth.

Scripted Introduction

If possible, share this introduction while you are outside on a sunny day. Begin by asking to the students:

? "When we look up in the sky during the day, what do we see?

Give the students time to answer, and point out the sun if they do not. (Caution—*DO NOT look directly at the sun because it can damage your eyes.*)

That's right! The sun plays a very important role for our Earth. It gives us light during the day and provides just the right amount of heat for our planet.

The energy created by lots of explosions on the sun heats up our Earth. We can also capture this solar energy and use it for power!

This week, we are going to look closer at the sun.

Read–Alouds

Encyclopedia Pages

- *The Usborne Children's Encyclopedia* pp. 262-263 "The Sun"

Library Books to Look For

- *The Sun: Our Nearest Star* (Let's-Read-and-Find Out) by Franklyn M. Branley and Edward Miller
- *Wake Up, Sun!* (Step-Into-Reading, Step 1) by David L. Harrison
- *The Sun Is My Favorite Star* by Frank Asch

Do – Hands-on Projects

Scientific Demonstration: Solar Melt

Materials Needed

- ✓ Muffin tin
- ✓ Foil
- ✓ Clear plastic wrap
- ✓ Marshmallows
- ✓ Chocolate chips
- ✓ Butter (or margarine)

Steps to Complete

1. Read the following introduction to your students:

   Remember earlier we talked about how the sun has lots of energy? And that energy helps to heat up our Earth? Now, we are going to harness that energy!

2. Have the students line three of the muffin cups with foil.

3. Then, have them place marshmallows in one cup, the chocolate in another cup, and the butter in the final cup. (Note—*You can line additional cups with foil and let the students choose other types of food to place in the remaining cups if desired.*)

4. Next, tightly wrap plastic wrap over the top of the pan, and set it outside in direct sunlight.

5. After 30 minutes check to see the differences. (Note—*The changes can take up to two hours to melt sufficiently depending on how hot the day is and how clear the day is.*)

6. Once you see changes taking place, ask the students:

   ? What happened to the marshmallows, chocolate, and butter?

Explanation

Read the following explaination to the students:

We saw the marshmallow, chocolate, and butter softened and melted after sitting out in the sun. The rays from the sun contain energy in the form of light and heat. This energy from the sun makes life possible on Earth. It also helps to create weather on our planet by heating up air and water on the surface.

Nature Study: Sunny Observations

This week, you are going to observe the effects of the sun. (Caution—*DO NOT look directly at the sun because it can damage your eyes.*)

Preparation

⟲ Read pp. 834-838 in the *Handbook of Nature Study* to learn more about the sun.

Outdoor Time

Go on a walk with the students to observe the effects of the sun. Stand in the shade, and then stand in the full sun. Observe how different it feels. You can use the information you have learned from reading the *Handbook of Nature Study* to answer the their questions or to share information about what they are observing.

Coordinating Activities

✂ Art – (Tissue Paper Sun) Give the students several squares of red, yellow, and orange tissue paper and a piece of paper with the outline of the sun. Have them glue the tissue paper sheets on the sun outline, overlapping them to create their own sun design. (Note—*You could also cut the tissue paper in circles instead if you want to emphasize the shape of a circle.*)

✂ Snack – (Sun Slices) Peel and slice an orange horizontally to form circles. Tell the students they are slices of the sun. Eat and enjoy!

✂ Activity – (Sun Pictures) SunPrint paper is blue paper that turns white when exposed to the sun. It can be purchased at your local craft store or online. When you cover a portion of the SunPrint paper, that part will remain blue, whereas the part exposed to the sun turns white, creating a picture. Have the students lay out their design on the paper according to the directions that come with the paper. Then, lay the paper out in the sun and watch their creations develop.

Write – Simple Notebooking

Student Diary

☐ Main Idea Page – Have the students color the coloring page found on SD p. 87.

☐ Demonstration Sheet – After you do the demonstration, fill out the demonstration sheet found on SD p. 88 with the students.

☐ Nature Journal Sheet – After you have your nature study time, fill out the nature journal sheet found on SD p. 89 with the students. The students can sketch what they have seen, or you can write down their observations.

☐ Art Page – Have the students use SD p. 90 to complete the art activity.

Lapbooking Templates

📁 Weekly Mini-book – Have the students cut out and color the Sun Mini-book on LT p. 39. You can have them cut out the main idea graphic included and glue it in the interior of the mini-book, or you can write a sentence with what they have learned from the week for them on the inside of the mini-book. Once the students are done, have them glue the booklet into the mini-lapbook.

📁 Overall Lapbook – Have the students cut out the "My Meteorology Projects" pocket on LT p. 45. Have them glue the pocket into the lapbook and add the coloring project they did to the pocket.

Week 2: The Water Cycle

2-Days-a-Week Schedule		
	Day 1	**Day 2**
Read	❑ Read the introduction with the students ❑ Read the selected pages in *The Usborne Children's Encyclopedia*	❑ Choose one or more of the additional books to read from this week
Do	❑ Complete the Scientific Demonstration "Water Cycle in a Jar" ❑ Eat "Clouds" for snack	❑ Complete the Nature Study "Dewy Observations" ❑ Do the "Raindrop Painting" activity
Write	❑ Color the main idea page ❑ Fill out the demonstration sheet	❑ Fill out the nature journal sheet ❑ Complete the art page

5-Days-a-Week Schedule					
	Day 1	**Day 2**	**Day 3**	**Day 4**	**Day 5**
Read	❑ Read the introduction with the students	❑ Read the selected pages in *The Usborne Children's Encyclopedia*	❑ Choose one or more of the additional books to read from this week	❑ Choose one or more of the additional books to read from this week	
Do	❑ Eat "Clouds" for snack	❑ Complete the Scientific Demonstration "Water Cycle in a Jar"	❑ Work on the activity "Cloud Matching"	❑ Do the "Raindrop Painting" activity	❑ Complete the Nature Study "Dewy Observations"
Write	❑ Color the main idea page	❑ Fill out the demonstration sheet	❑ Complete the Water Cycle Mini-book	❑ Complete the art page	❑ Fill out the nature journal sheet

Read – Information Gathering

Weekly Topic

⚡ The water cycle shows the movement of water on the Earth.

Scripted Introduction

Have a picture of the water cycle on the table in front of you. You can find a template of the water cycle in the appendix on p. 192. Say to the students:

> The amount of water on the Earth never changes. It just switches forms above and below the Earth. We show the movement of water on the Earth with something called the water cycle.

Point to the picture of the water cycle. (Note—*As you go through the next five steps, point to the place the step is shown on the water cycle sheet.*) Say to the students:

> The water cycle begins with water in the oceans and the seas. The sun heats up the water in the seas, lakes, and oceans around the Earth.

> Next, invisible drops of water called water vapor, rise up into the air. Then, these water vapor drops combine together and form clouds. When the drops in the clouds get very heavy, they fall to the ground as rain or snow.

> This water runs back into rivers, lakes, and oceans to be heated up by the sun again! This week, we are going to learn more about water vapor and the water cycle.

Read–Alouds

Encyclopedia Pages

📖 *The Usborne Children's Encyclopedia* p. 14 "The Weather"

Library Books to Look For

📖 *The Water Cycle* (First Facts, Water All Around) by Rebecca Olien
📖 *The Magic School Bus Wet All Over: A Book About The Water Cycle* by Pat Relf and Carolyn Bracken

Do – Hands-on Projects

Scientific Demonstration: Water Cycle in a Jar

Materials Needed

✓ Clear glass jar

✓ Jar lid or bowl
✓ Ice cubes
✓ Hot water

Steps to Complete

1. Read the following introduction to your students:

   Remember earlier we saw a picture of the water cycle? Now, we are going to see it in action!

2. Fill the jar two-thirds of the way full with hot water. (Note—*The jar will get very warm, so do not leave the students unsupervised at any point during this project!*)

3. Have the students quickly cover the jar with a bowl or an upside down jar lid. Have them fill the lid and bowl with ice cubes.

4. Observe the changes that take place over the next thirty minutes.

Explanation

Read the following explaination to the students:

We saw condensation forming after a few minutes. Eventually we saw droplets form and fall in the jar. The conditions created in the jar are similar to the ones that produce storms and rain on Earth. The warm, moist air comes in contact with cool air. Then, the water vapor condenses, collects, and falls.

Nature Study: Dewy Observations

This week, you are going to observe water vapor in the form of dew. (Note—*If you are lucky enough to have a rain storm this week, have the students observe the clouds and the ground before and after the storm.*)

Preparation

↪ Read pp. 808-814 in the *Handbook of Nature Study* to learn more about the forms of water in nature.

Outdoor Time

Go on a walk with the students early in the morning to observe the dew on the ground. Allow the students to make observations about what they find. You can use the information you have learned from reading the *Handbook of Nature Study* to answer their questions or to share information about what they are observing.

Coordinating Activities

✂ Art – (Raindrop Painting) Give the students a small spray bottle or eyedropper with blue paint that has been diluted with water. Have them rain down the paint (i.e., squirt) onto a sheet of paper.

✂ Snack — (Clouds) Make a few clouds for the students to eat. Beat 2 egg whites with ¼ tsp of cream of tartar until stiff peaks form. Add in ½ tsp vanilla and ⅓ cup sugar. Beat until well incorporated. Drop spoonfuls on a cookie sheet lined with foil. Bake at 325°F for 10 minutes, then turn off the oven. (Note—*Don't open the oven door.*) Let the clouds sit in the oven for 50 more minutes. Remove and serve.

✂ Activity — (Cloud Matching) Have the students match clouds by color and/or by size. Cut out the clouds on the Cloud Matching sheet found in the appendix on p. 193 to use for this activity.

Write – Simple Notebooking

Student Diary

☐ Main Idea Page — Have the students color the coloring page found on SD p. 91.

☐ Demonstration Sheet — After you do the demonstration, fill out the demonstration sheet found on SD p. 92 with the students.

☐ Nature Journal Sheet — After you have your nature study time, fill out the nature journal sheet found on SD p. 93 with the students. The students can sketch what they have seen, or you can write down their observations.

☐ Art Page — Have the students use SD p. 94 to complete the art activity.

Lapbooking Templates

🗀 Weekly Mini-book — Have the students cut out and color the Water Cycle Mini-book on LT p. 40. You can have them cut out the main idea graphic included and glue it in the interior of the mini-book, or you can write a sentence with what they have learned from the week for them on the inside of the mini-book. Once the students are done, have them glue the booklet into the mini-lapbook.

🗀 Overall Lapbook — Have the students add the page they painted to the "My Meteorology Projects" pocket in the lapbook.

Week 3: The Seasons

2-Days-a-Week Schedule		
	Day 1	**Day 2**
Read	❑ Read the introduction with the students ❑ Read the selected pages in *The Usborne Children's Encyclopedia*	❑ Choose one or more of the additional books to read from this week
Do	❑ Start the Scientific Demonstration "Weather Watch" (*This will continue through the week.*) ❑ Eat "Banana Snowmen" for snack	❑ Work on demonstration ❑ Complete the Nature Study "Seasonal Tree Study" ❑ Do the "Seasons Collage" activity
Write	❑ Color the main idea page ❑ Fill out the demonstration sheet	❑ Fill out the nature journal sheet ❑ Complete the art page

5-Days-a-Week Schedule					
	Day 1	**Day 2**	**Day 3**	**Day 4**	**Day 5**
Read	❑ Read the introduction with the students	❑ Read the selected pages in *The Usborne Children's Encyclopedia*	❑ Choose one or more of the additional books to read from this week	❑ Choose one or more of the additional books to read from this week	
Do	❑ Start the Scientific Demonstration "Weather Watch" (*This will continue through the week.*)	❑ Eat "Banana Snowmen" for snack ❑ Work on demonstration	❑ Work on the activity "Seasons Book" ❑ Work on demonstration	❑ Do the "Seasons Collage" activity ❑ Work on demonstration	❑ Complete the Nature Study "Seasonal Tree Study" ❑ Work on demonstration
Write	❑ Color the main idea page	❑ Fill out the demonstration sheet	❑ Complete the Seasons Mini-book	❑ Complete the art page	❑ Fill out the nature journal sheet

Read – Information Gathering

Weekly Topic

♪ Spring, summer, fall, and winter are all seasons.

Scripted Introduction

Say to the students:

A season is a collection of days with a typical weather pattern. On Earth, we have four seasons—spring, summer, fall, and winter.

Typically, winter has shorter days that can be filled with cold and snow. Around spring it warms, and flowers begin to bloom. During summer, the days are longer and hotter. And finally, fall is marked by a drop in the temperature and a change in the leaves.

? Can you guess what season it is now?

Allow the students to answer, and provide them with the correct season if they do not guess it. Then, say to the students:

Winter, spring, summer, and fall are all seasons. This week, we are going to learn more about the seasons.

Read–Alouds

Encyclopedia Pages

📖 *The Usborne Children's Encyclopedia* pp. 12-13 "The Seasons"

Library Books to Look For

📖 *Watching the Seasons* (Welcome Books) by Edana Eckart
📖 *Sunshine Makes the Seasons* (Let's-Read-and-Find... Science 2) by Franklyn M. Branley and Michael Rex
📖 *Our Seasons* by Ranida T. Mckneally and Grace Lin

Do – Hands-on Projects

Scientific Demonstration: Weather Watch

Materials Needed

✓ Weather stickers (appendix p. 194)

Steps to Complete

1. Read the following introduction to your students:

   Remember earlier we talked about the four seasons and how each season typically has different weather? Now, we are going to spend time this week observing our weather!

2. Have the students observe the weather each day for five days.

3. Each day, have them glue the appropriate weather watch stickers on the chart found in student diary. Each day, ask the students:

   ? What is the weather like today?

Explanation

The students should see a variety of weather over the week.

Nature Study: Seasonal Tree Study

This week, you will begin a seasonal tree study.

Preparation

↻ Read pp. 618-625 in the *Handbook of Nature Study* to learn more about trees and tree study.

Outdoor Time

Go on a walk with the students to choose a tree they want to study in each season. Allow the students to make observations about what they find. You can use the information you have learned from reading the *Handbook of Nature Study* to answer their questions or to share information about what they are observing. When you get home, make an entry into their nature journal for the current season you are in. (Note—*Continue this tree study for the remaining three seasons over the year.*)

Coordinating Activities

✂ Art – (Seasons Collage) Make a collage for the season you are in using pictures from magazines. For example, if you do this week during the winter, use pictures of snowflakes, bare trees, icicles, Christmas trees, and so on. Have the students glue the pictures on a sheet of paper as a collage.

✂ Snack – (Banana Snowmen) Use bananas, grapes, strawberries, raisins, carrots, and skewers to make snowmen on a stick. You can see directions for this here:

   ☞ http://onehandedcooks.com.au/recipe/christmas-banana-snowmen/

✂ Activity – (Seasons Book) Have the students make a book depicting the different seasons. You will need the following supplies: paper, crayons, and staples. Have the students make a book with a page for each season. Have them draw their own pictures of the different activities or the things they see in a particular season. You can download a template for a book like this here:

🖰 https://elementalscience.com/blogs/science-activities/seasons-hawk-talons

Write – Simple Notebooking

Student Diary

- ☐ Main Idea Page – Have the students color the coloring page found on SD p. 95.
- ☐ Demonstration Sheet – Add the daily weather stickers to SD p. 96 with the students.
- ☐ Nature Journal Sheet – After you have your nature study time, fill out the nature journal sheet found on SD p. 97 with the students. The students can sketch what they have seen, or you can write down their observations. (Note—*When you do this project again in a few months you can use the same nature journal sheet.*)
- ☐ Art Page – Have the students use SD p. 98 to complete the art activity.

Lapbooking Templates

- ☐ Weekly Mini-book – Have the students cut out and color the Seasons Mini-book on LT p. 41. You can have them cut out the main idea graphic included and glue it in the interior of the mini-book, or you can write a sentence with what they have learned from the week for them on the inside of the mini-book. Once the students are done, have them glue the booklet into the mini-lapbook.
- ☐ Overall Lapbook – Have the students add the page they painted to the "My Meteorology Projects" pocket in the lapbook.

Week 4: Wind

	2-Days-a-Week Schedule	
	Day 1	**Day 2**
Read	❏ Read the introduction with the students ❏ Read the selected pages in *The Usborne Children's Encyclopedia*	❏ Choose one or more of the additional books to read from this week
Do	❏ Complete the Scientific Demonstration "Capture Wind" ❏ Eat "Jell-O Storms" for snack	❏ Complete the Nature Study "Wind" ❏ Do the "Draw a Storm" activity
Write	❏ Color the main idea page ❏ Fill out the demonstration sheet	❏ Fill out the nature journal sheet ❏ Complete the art page

	5-Days-a-Week Schedule				
	Day 1	**Day 2**	**Day 3**	**Day 4**	**Day 5**
Read	❏ Read the introduction with the students	❏ Read the selected pages in *The Usborne Children's Encyclopedia*	❏ Choose one or more of the additional books to read from this week	❏ Choose one or more of the additional books to read from this week	
Do	❏ Eat "Jell-O Storms" for snack	❏ Complete the Scientific Demonstration "Capture Wind"	❏ Work on the activity "Weather Mobile"	❏ Do the "Draw a Storm" activity	❏ Complete the Nature Study "Wind"
Write	❏ Color the main idea page	❏ Fill out the demonstration sheet	❏ Complete the Wind Mini-book	❏ Complete the art page	❏ Fill out the nature journal sheet

Read – Information Gathering

Weekly Topic

ᕯ When air moves it causes wind.

Scripted Introduction

If possible, share this introduction while you are outside on a windy day. Say to the students:

When air moves, it causes what we know as wind.

? Can you think of a sign of a windy day?

Let the students share a few ideas, and then say to the students:

Those are good ideas. When it's windy out, we can see the grass and leaves blow. The tree branches bend and sway.

Wind is caused by the uneven heating of the surface of the Earth. As the sun heats up the surface and the air around it, the warm air rises. This uneven heating causes air to move around, creating wind.

This week, we are going to spend some time learning about wind.

Read-Alouds

Encyclopedia Pages

▭ *The Usborne Children's Encyclopedia* p. 15 "Windy Weather"

Library Books to Look For

▭ *Feel the Wind* (Let's-Read-and-Find... Science 2) by Arthur Dorros
▭ *The Wind Blew* by Pat Hutchins
▭ *Can You See the Wind?* (Rookie Read-About Science) by Allan Fowler

Do – Hands-on Projects

Scientific Demonstration: Capture Wind

Materials Needed

✓ Bubble mixture

Note—You can make your own bubble solution by following the directions found here:

🖱 https://artfulparent.com/how-to-make-homemade-bubbles/

✓ Bubble wand

Steps to Complete

1. Read the following introduction to your students:

   Remember earlier we learned about wind? Now, we are going to capture our own wind!

2. Have the students dip the bubble wand into the bubble mixture so that it coats the inside of the ring.

3. Have them gently blow on the bubble wand so that bubbles form, capturing their wind.

4. Have the students observe the bubbles as they form and watch where they go.

Explanation

Read the following explaination to the students:

We saw our breath captured as the bubbles form. Wind is just moving air, so on a breazy day, we could do the same! We could capture wind with the bubbles.

Nature Study: Wind

This week, you will observe the wind. (Note—*If you do not have a breezy day, wait until you do have one to do this nature study.*)

Preparation

↪ Read pp. 791-798 in the *Handbook of Nature Study* to learn more about the winds of the world.

Outdoor Time

Go on a walk with the students to observe the signs of wind. Allow the students to make observations about what they find. You can use the information you have learned from reading the *Handbook of Nature Study* to answer their questions or to share information about what they are observing.

Coordinating Activities

✂ **Art** – (Draw a Storm) Have the students draw a picture of a storm on a piece of paper. Let their imaginations run free for this project!

✂ **Snack** – (Jell-O Storms) Make your favorite blue-colored Jell-O, and fill a clear cup halfway with it for the rain. Then, top the rain Jell-O off with Cool Whip for clouds! (Note—*You could use food coloring to tint the Cool Whip gray for more authentic rain clouds.*)

✂ **Activity** – (Weather Mobile) Have the students make a mobile showing the different types of weather. You will need string, two sticks, and a copy of the weather sticker templates found in the appendix on p. 194. Begin by having the students choose two sticks from outside for a mobile. Have them color the weather mobile templates, while you secure their two sticks together with string in a X shape. Then punch holes in each of the weather pictures, and add one to each of the four ends of the sticks.

Write – Simple Notebooking

Student Diary

- ☐ Main Idea Page – Have the students color the coloring page found on SD p. 99.
- ☐ Demonstration Sheet – After you do the demonstration, fill out the demonstration sheet found on SD p. 100 with the students.
- ☐ Nature Journal Sheet – After you have your nature study time, fill out the nature journal sheet found on SD p. 101 with the students. The students can sketch what they have seen, or you can write down their observations.
- ☐ Art Page – Have the students use SD p. 102 to complete the art activity.

Lapbooking Templates

- 🗁 Weekly Mini-book – Have the students cut out and color the Wind Mini-book on LT p. 42. You can have them cut out the main idea graphic included and glue it in the interior of the mini-book, or you can write a sentence with what they have learned from the week for them on the inside of the mini-book. Once the students are done, have them glue the booklet into the mini-lapbook.
- 🗁 Overall Lapbook – Have the students add the page they painted to the "My Meteorology Projects" pocket in the lapbook.

Week 5: Tornadoes

2-Days-a-Week Schedule		
	Day 1	**Day 2**
Read	❑ Read the introduction with the students ❑ Read the selected pages in *The Usborne Children's Encyclopedia*	❑ Choose one or more of the additional books to read from this week
Do	❑ Complete the Scientific Demonstration "Tornado in a Jar" ❑ Eat "Tornado Smoothies" for snack	❑ Complete the Nature Study "Tornadoes" ❑ Do the "Swirling Art" activity
Write	❑ Color the main idea page ❑ Fill out the demonstration sheet	❑ Fill out the nature journal sheet ❑ Complete the art page

5-Days-a-Week Schedule				
	Day 1	**Day 2**	**Day 3**	**Day 4**	**Day 5**
Read	❑ Read the introduction with the students	❑ Read the selected pages in *The Usborne Children's Encyclopedia*	❑ Choose one or more of the additional books to read from this week	❑ Choose one or more of the additional books to read from this week	
Do	❑ Eat "Tornado Smoothies" for snack	❑ Complete the Scientific Demonstration "Tornado in a Jar"	❑ Work on the activity "Another Twister"	❑ Do the "Swirling Art" activity	❑ Complete the Nature Study "Tornadoes"
Write	❑ Color the main idea page	❑ Fill out the demonstration sheet	❑ Complete the Tornado Mini-book	❑ Complete the art page	❑ Fill out the nature journal sheet

Read – Information Gathering

Weekly Topic

- Tornadoes are funnels of spinning wind.

Scripted Introduction

Have pictures of tornadoes, either from magazines or off the Internet, on the table in front of you. Say to the students:

> These are all pictures of tornadoes. Tornadoes are funnels of spinning wind that touch the ground and are connected to the clouds above.

> Most tornadoes only last a few minutes, but in that time they can tear up trees and houses, plus move cars, animals, and people.

> They typically form in the spring in the middle of a very strong storm. This week, we are going to learn more about tornadoes.

(Note—*If you live in a tornado-prone area, this would be a good week to learn more about tornado safety.*)

Read-Alouds

Encyclopedia Pages

- *The Usborne Children's Encyclopedia* pp. 16-17 "Storms and Floods"

Library Books to Look For

- *Tornado Alert* (Let's-Read-and-Find… Science 2) by Franklyn M. Branley and Giulio Maestro
- *Tornadoes!* (DK Readers) by DK Publishing
- *The Terrifying Tub Tornado* by Ann K. Larson

Do – Hands-on Projects

Scientific Demonstration: Tornado in a Jar

Materials Needed

- ✓ Pint-sized Mason jar
- ✓ Dish soap
- ✓ Vinegar
- ✓ Water
- ✓ Glitter

Steps to Complete

1. Read the following introduction to your students:

   Remember earlier we looked at tornadoes? Now, we are going to recreate one in a jar!

2. Make the tornado solution by mixing 1 ½ cups of water, half a teaspoon of dish soap, and half of a teaspoon of vinegar. Then, pour the solution into the Mason jar.

3. Have the students add a bit of glitter before you tighten on the lid.

4. Place one hand on the bottom of the jar and the other hand on the top. Then, swirl the jar in a circular motion for a few seconds.

5. Set the jar down on a flat surface, and have the students observe what happens. Ask them:

   ? What do you see happening in the jar?

Explanation

Read the following explaination to the students:

We saw a mini-tornado form in our jar! When we swirled the jar in a circle, the water started rotating and formed a vortex that looks like a tornado.

Nature Study: Tornadoes

This week, you won't be heading outside to observe tornadoes because that would be too dangerous! Instead, you will be looking at a website about tornadoes and then creating a journal page with what the students have learned. If you do have a thunderstorm this week, take a moment to observe it from the inside of your home.

Preparation

⌔ Look over the website below to determine what parts of it you want to highlight.

Outdoor Time

☼ Spend some time on this website to learn more about tornadoes:
http://www.weatherwizkids.com/weather-tornado.htm

Coordinating Activities

✂ Art – (Swirling Art) Give the students a thick paintbrush, a piece of paper, and some black and white paint on a plate. Have them get a bit of black and white paint on the paintbrush and make swirls on the paper until they have created a gray, swirly tornado.

✂ Snack – (Tornado Smoothies) Blend ½ cup of your favorite frozen fruit (strawberries or peaches), ½ cup of ice cream, and ½ cup milk or juice. First, blend the fruit and milk together until well blended, then add the ice cream and whip until smooth.

✂ **Activity** – (Another Twister) Have the students make another tornado at home. You will need two clear plastic bottles, a washer, and duct tape. The directions for this activity can be found at:

🖱 https://www.mombrite.com/tornado-in-a-bottle/

Write – Simple Notebooking

Student Diary

☐ **Main Idea Page** – Have the students color the coloring page found on SD p. 103.

☐ **Demonstration Sheet** – After you do the demonstration, fill out the demonstration sheet found on SD p. 104 with the students.

☐ **Nature Journal Sheet** – After you have your nature study time, fill out the nature journal sheet found on SD p. 105 with the students. The students can sketch what they have seen, or you can write down their observations.

☐ **Art Page** – Have the students use SD p. 106 to complete the art activity.

Lapbooking Templates

📁 **Weekly Mini-book** – Have the students cut out and color the Tornado Mini-book on LT p. 43. You can have them cut out the main idea graphic included and glue it in the interior of the mini-book, or you can write a sentence with what they have learned from the week for them on the inside of the mini-book. Once the students are done, have them glue the booklet into the mini-lapbook.

📁 **Overall Lapbook** – Have the students add the page they painted to the "My Meteorology Projects" pocket in the lapbook.

Week 6: Thermometer

2-Days-a-Week Schedule		
	Day 1	**Day 2**
Read	❑ Read the introduction with the students ❑ Read the selected pages in *The Usborne Children's Encyclopedia*	❑ Choose one or more of the additional books to read from this week
Do	❑ Complete the Scientific Demonstration "Hot and Cold" ❑ Eat "Hot and Cold" for snack	❑ Complete the Nature Study "Temperature and Thermometers" ❑ Do the "Temperature Collage" activity
Write	❑ Color the main idea page ❑ Fill out the demonstration sheet	❑ Fill out the nature journal sheet ❑ Complete the art page

5-Days-a-Week Schedule				
	Day 1	**Day 2**	**Day 3**	**Day 4**	**Day 5**
Read	❑ Read the introduction with the students	❑ Read the selected pages in *The Usborne Children's Encyclopedia*	❑ Choose one or more of the additional books to read from this week	❑ Choose one or more of the additional books to read from this week	
Do	❑ Eat "Hot and Cold" for snack	❑ Complete the Scientific Demonstration "Hot and Cold"	❑ Work on the activity "Homemade Thermometer"	❑ Do the "Temperature Collage" activity	❑ Complete the Nature Study "Temperature and Thermometers"
Write	❑ Color the main idea page	❑ Fill out the demonstration sheet	❑ Complete the Thermometer Mini-book	❑ Complete the art page	❑ Fill out the nature journal sheet

Read – Information Gathering

Weekly Topic

🐾 A thermometer tells us whether it is hot or cold.

Scripted Introduction

Have a thermometer on the table in front of you. Say to the students:

> This is a thermometer. It's job is to tell us whether it is hot or cold.

Demonstrate to the students how to read a thermometer. Then place your finger over the bulb at the bottom of the thermometer to heat it up.

> **?** Can you see how the line rises when I heat it up with my thumb?

> The higher the line on a thermometer is, the hotter it is. The lower the line on the thermometer is, the colder it is.

> This week, we are going to learn more about thermometers.

Read–Alouds

Encyclopedia Pages

📖 *The Usborne Children's Encyclopedia* pp. 196-197 "Hot and Cold"

Library Books to Look For

📖 *What Is a Thermometer* (Rookie Read-About Science) by Lisa Trumbauer
📖 *Thermometers* (First Facts. Science Tools) by Adele Richardson
📖 *Temperature* (Blastoff! Readers, First Science) by Kay Manolis
📖 *Too, Too Hot* (Reader's Clubhouse Level 1 Reader) by Judy Kentor Schmauss

Do – Hands-on Projects

Scientific Demonstration: Hot and Cold

Materials Needed

- ✓ 2 Clear cups
- ✓ Food coloring
- ✓ Water (hot and ice-cold)
- ✓ Thermometer

Steps to Complete

1. Read the following introduction to your students:

   Remember earlier we saw how a thermometer can tell us when it is hot or cold? Now, we are going to see how temperature can affect movement!

2. {**Adults Only**} Fill one cup about halfway with hot water. Fill the other cup about halfway with ice-cold water. Then, help the students take the temperature of each and record that on their demonstration sheet.

3. Have the students add a few drops of food coloring into each cup. Then, set a timer for one minute and observe how well the color mixes into the water.

4. Repeat the observation every minute with the students.

Explanation

Read the following explaination to the students:

   We saw that the color mixed quicker into the hot water than it did in the cold water. This is because the color molecules move quicker when it's warm.

Nature Study: Temperature and Thermometers

This week, you will be examining outdoor temperatures.

Preparation

↻ Read pp. 790-791 in the *Handbook of Nature Study* to learn more about temperature and thermometers.

Outdoor Time

Go on a walk with the students to observe the temperature and how it makes you feel. Be sure to find a thermometer (or bring your own) to observe while on your walk. You can use the information you have learned from reading the *Handbook of Nature Study* to answer their questions or to share information about what they are observing.

Coordinating Activities

✂ Art – (Temperature Collage) Have the students cut out magazine pictures or use stickers to make their collage. On one half of a sheet of paper or poster board, have them paste pictures of things you do or use when it is hot. On the other half, have them paste pictures of things you do or use when it is cold.

✂ Snack – (Hot and Cold) Choose two or three warm foods, such as tea or soup, and two or three cold foods, such as cheese or ice cream. Have the students use a food thermometer (not a mercury thermometer) to test the temperature of each food. Then eat the food as you talk about the differences.

✂ **Activity** – (Homemade Thermometer) Make a thermometer with the students. You will need modeling clay, food coloring, water, a clear straw, rubbing alcohol, and a small clear bottle with a narrow neck. The directions for the activity can be found at:

🖱 https://teachbesideme.com/homemade-thermometer-science-experiment/

Write – Simple Notebooking

Student Diary

- ☐ **Main Idea Page** – Have the students color the coloring page found on SD p. 107.

- ☐ **Demonstration Sheet** – As you do the demonstrations, record the students observations on SD p. 108 with the students.

- ☐ **Nature Journal Sheet** – After you have your nature study time, fill out the nature journal sheet found on SD p. 109 with the students. The students can sketch what they have seen, or you can write down their observations.

- ☐ **Art Page** – Have the students use SD p. 110 to complete the art activity.

Lapbooking Templates

- 📁 **Weekly Mini-book** – Have the students cut out and color the Thermometer Mini-book on LT p. 44. You can have them cut out the main idea graphic included and glue it in the interior of the mini-book, or you can write a sentence with what they have learned from the week for them on the inside of the mini-book. Once the students are done, have them glue the booklet into the mini-lapbook.

- 📁 **Overall Lapbook** – Have the students add the page they painted to the "My Meteorology Projects" pocket in the lapbook.

Intro to Science

Unit 5: Intro to Botany

Intro to Botany Unit Overview

Sequence for Study

- Week 1: Plants
- Week 2: Flowers
- Week 3: Seeds
- Week 4: Leaves
- Week 5: Stems
- Week 6: Roots

Supplies Needed for the Unit

Week	Introduction Props	Hands-on Project Materials	Coordinating Activities Supplies
1	Small potted plant	Small pot, Bean seed, Potting soil, Water	Potato or carrot sticks, Celery, Lettuce, Berries, Tissue paper squares (brown, green, red, and purple), Glue, Paper
2	Plant with a flower	Tulip, Razor or knife, Magnifying glass, Q-tip	Cake with icing flowers, A large White T-shirt (100% cotton), Cardboard, Flowers and Leaves, Masking Tape, Newspaper or Towels, Hammer, Paint, Paper
3	Lima bean seed (soaked overnight)	3 Bean seeds, Paper towel, Plastic baggie, Tape, and Water	Different fruits and seeds to eat, Red paint, Apple, Plate, Paper, Paintbrush, Glue, Seeds
4	Bean plant	Bean plant, Paper, Paper clip	Edible leaves (lettuce, spinach, kale or bok choy), Ranch dressing, Sheet of cardboard, Leaves, Crayons, Paper, Leaves, Tape, Newspaper, Hammer
5	Celery, Magnifying glass	Celery (with leaves), Food coloring, Glass, Water	Celery Sticks, Cream Cheese, Brown and green paint, Straw, Water, Paper
6	Green onion with roots	Green onion, Cup, Water	Green onion with roots, Carrot sticks or shoestring potato sticks, Green onion with roots, Paint, Paper

Books Scheduled

Hands-on Projects

- *Handbook of Nature Study (If you are using the nature study option.)*

Scheduled Encyclopedias

- *The Usborne Children's Encyclopedia*

Library Books to Look For

Week 1
- *From Seed to Plant* (Rookie Read-About Science) by Allan Fowler
- *From Seed to Plant* by Gail Gibbons

Week 2
- *The Reason for a Flower* (Ruth Heller's World of Nature) by Ruth Heller
- *Planting a Rainbow* by Lois Ehler

Week 3
- *The Magic School Bus Plants Seeds: A Book About How Living Things Grow* by Joanna Cole
- *Seeds* by Ken Robbins
- *A Fruit Is a Suitcase for Seeds* by Jean Richards and Anca Hariton
- *Curious George Plants a Seed* (Curious George Early Readers) by H. A. Rey

Week 4
- *Leaves* (Plant Parts series) (Pebble Plus: Plant Parts) by Vijaya Bodach,
- *I Am A Leaf* (Level 1 – Hello Reader) by Jean Marzollo and Judith Moffatt
- *Leaves* by David Ezra Stein

Week 5
- *Stems* (Plant Parts) by Vijaya Bodach
- *Plant Stems & Roots* (Look Once, Look Again Science Series) by David M. Schwartz
- *Stems* (First Step Nonfiction) by Melanie Mitchell

Week 6
- *Roots* (First Step Nonfiction) by Melanie Mitchell
- *Roots* (Plant Parts series) (Pebble Plus: Plant Parts) by Vijaya Bodach
- *Plant Plumbing: A Book About Roots and Stems* by Susan Blackaby

Week 1: Plants

You do not need to complete all of this in a week. Instead, choose from the following options.

2-Days-a-Week Schedule		
	Day 1	**Day 2**
Read	❑ Read the introduction with the students ❑ Read the selected pages in *The Usborne Children's Encyclopedia*	❑ Choose one or more of the additional books to read from this week
Do	❑ Start the Scientific Demonstration "Plant Growth" ❑ Eat "Edible Plants" for snack	❑ Complete the Nature Study "Plants" ❑ Do the "Mosaic Plants" activity ❑ Observe the Plant's Growth
Write	❑ Color the main idea page ❑ Fill out the demonstration sheet	❑ Fill out the nature journal sheet ❑ Complete the art page

5-Days-a-Week Schedule					
	Day 1	**Day 2**	**Day 3**	**Day 4**	**Day 5**
Read	❑ Read the introduction with the students	❑ Read the selected pages in *The Usborne Children's Encyclopedia*	❑ Choose one or more of the additional books to read from this week	❑ Choose one or more of the additional books to read from this week	
Do	❑ Eat "Edible Plants" for snack	❑ Start the Scientific Demonstration "Plant Growth"	❑ Work on the activity "Bean Plant"	❑ Do the "Mosaic Plants" activity	❑ Complete the Nature Study "Plants" ❑ Observe the Plant's Growth
Write	❑ Color the main idea page	❑ Fill out the demonstration sheet	❑ Complete the Plants Mini-book	❑ Complete the art page	❑ Fill out the nature journal sheet

Read – Information Gathering

Weekly Topic

- Plants grow toward the light.

Scripted Introduction

Have a small potted plant out on the table in front of you. Say to the students:

> Let's take a look at this plant.

> **?** What do you notice about it?

You can ask questions like what color is it, how does it feel, what does it smell like, if the students need more guidance for their observations.

> Those are great observations! Plants use light, water, and air to make food. We call the process they use to make food photosynthesis.

> And because plants need light to make food, they will typically grow toward the light. Doing this makes it easier for them to get the sunlight they need to make food.

> This week, we are going to look closer at plants.

Over the next several weeks, you will look at the different parts of a plant, but you may want to introduce them now (i.e., roots, stem, leaves, flowers, and fruit).

Read-Alouds

Encyclopedia Pages

- *The Usborne Children's Encyclopedia* p. 92 "Plant World"

Library Books to Look For

- *From Seed to Plant* (Rookie Read-About Science) by Allan Fowler
- *From Seed to Plant* by Gail Gibbons

Do – Hands-on Projects

Scientific Demonstration: Plant Growth

Materials Needed

- ✓ Small pot
- ✓ Bean seed

✓ Potting soil
✓ Water

Steps to Complete

1. Read the following introduction to your students:

   Remember earlier we looked at a potted plant? Now, we are going to plant one and watch it grow!

2. Have the students fill the pot with soil and make an indention in the soil large enough for the seed.

3. Have them place the seed in the hole and cover it with dirt. Give the seed a bit of water, and then set it in a safe place where it can sit undisturbed. (Note—*In week 4 of this unit, you will need a bean plant for the experiment, so you may want to do this activity this week to ensure that you have a bean plant for that week.*)

4. Over the rest of the week, have the students check their bean seeds each day and water them if the soil appears dry.

5. At the end of the week, ask the students:

   ? What happened to our bean seeds this week?

Explanation

Read the following explaination to the students:

   We saw the bean seed sprout, and a plant started to grow up from the soil and toward the light over the week. We are going to set our baby plant aside and watch it grow even more over the next few weeks.

Nature Study: Plants

This week, you will begin to look at the plants found in the habitat in which you live.

Preparation

↪ Read pp. 453-456 in the *Handbook of Nature Study* to learn more about plants and how to guide a study of plants in nature.

Outdoor Time

✿ Go on a walk and observe the different types of plants you see. If you can, take a walk in the woods to observe how plants tend to grow on the forest floor in places where more light gets through. Allow them to make additional observations while also guiding them to see that plants have leaves and stems.

Coordinating Activities

✂ **Art** – (Mosaic Plant) Cut up squares of different colors of tissue paper for the different plant parts, for example, brown for the stem, green for the leaves, red for the fruit, and purple for the flowers. Have the students ball up the paper and glue it onto a black-line image or drawing of a plant. When they are finished, have them color the sun above the flower to remind them that plants grow toward the light.

✂ **Snack** – (Edible Plants) Explain to the students that we eat many different types of plants and different parts of the plant—they are our vegetables and fruits! Then, let the students create a plant out of food. You can let them use potato or carrot sticks from the roots, celery for the stem, lettuce for the leaves, and berries for the fruit. Take a picture, then eat it all up!

✂ **Activity** – (Plant Growth Video) – Have the students watch the following video to see how plants grow:

🖱 https://www.youtube.com/watch?v=Xn-3PBM5-70

Write – Simple Notebooking

Student Diary

☐ **Main Idea Page** – Have the students color the coloring page found on SD p. 113.

☐ **Demonstration Sheet** – After you do the demonstration, fill out the demonstration sheet found on SD p. 114 with the students.

☐ **Nature Journal Sheet** – After you have your nature study time, fill out the nature journal sheet found on SD p. 115 with the students. The students can sketch what they have seen, or you can write down their observations.

☐ **Art Page** – Have the students use SD p. 116 to complete the art activity.

Lapbooking Templates

📁 **Weekly Mini-book** – Have the students cut out and color the Plants Mini-book on LT p. 49. You can have them cut out the main idea graphic included and glue it in the interior of the mini-book, or you can write a sentence with what they have learned from the week for them on the inside of the mini-book. Once the students are done, have them glue the booklet into the mini-lapbook.

📁 **Overall Lapbook** – Have the students cut out the "My Botany Projects" pocket on LT p. 55. Have them glue the pocket into the lapbook and add the coloring project they did to the pocket.

Week 2: Flowers

2-Days-a-Week Schedule		
	Day 1	**Day 2**
Read	❑ Read the introduction with the students ❑ Read the selected pages in *The Usborne Children's Encyclopedia*	❑ Choose one or more of the additional books to read from this week
Do	❑ Complete the Scientific Demonstration "Dissecting a Flower" ❑ Eat "Flower Cake" for snack	❑ Complete the Nature Study "Flowers" ❑ Do the "Field of Flowers" activity
Write	❑ Color the main idea page ❑ Fill out the demonstration sheet	❑ Fill out the nature journal sheet ❑ Complete the art page

5-Days-a-Week Schedule					
	Day 1	**Day 2**	**Day 3**	**Day 4**	**Day 5**
Read	❑ Read the introduction with the students	❑ Read the selected pages in *The Usborne Children's Encyclopedia*	❑ Choose one or more of the additional books to read from this week	❑ Choose one or more of the additional books to read from this week	
Do	❑ Eat "Flower Cake" for snack	❑ Complete the Scientific Demonstration "Dissecting a Flower"	❑ Work on the activity "Nature Prints"	❑ Do the "Field of Flowers" activity	❑ Complete the Nature Study "Flowers"
Write	❑ Color the main idea page	❑ Fill out the demonstration sheet	❑ Complete the Flowers Mini-book	❑ Complete the art page	❑ Fill out the nature journal sheet

Read – Information Gathering

Weekly Topic

- Flowers have the parts of a plant needed to make a seed.

Scripted Introduction

Have a plant with a flower out on the table in front of you. Look for a plant that has a full flower with the parts visible and if possible a bud that has not opened yet. (Note—*If you can't find a plant like this, you can use the labeled sketch on p. 195 of the appendix.*) Say to the students:

> This flower has all the parts of a plant that are needed to make a seed. After the flower is pollinated, it can produce a seed from which a baby plant can grow.

As you describe the different parts, point to them on your plant or on the sheet from the appendix.

> All flowers begin as buds. The bud open up and develops into a flower with petals to help attract insects toward the center of the flower. In the center of the flower are the parts of the plant, like the pistil and stamen, that are needed to make the seed.
>
> Insects or the wind move the pollen from the stamen to the top of the pistil of the flower. The pollen then travels down a tube in the pistil, and a seed is formed. We call this process pollination, and it's the main reason plants have flowers! This week, we are going to look closer at flowers.

Read–Alouds

Encyclopedia Pages

- *The Usborne Children's Encyclopedia* p. 93 "Flowering Plants"

Library Books to Look For

- *The Reason for a Flower* (Ruth Heller's World of Nature) by Ruth Heller
- *Planting a Rainbow* by Lois Ehler

Do – Hands-on Projects

Scientific Demonstration: Dissecting a Flower

Materials Needed

- ✓ Tulip (or other single flower with clearly defined parts)

✓ Razor or knife
✓ Magnifying glass
✓ Q-tip

Steps to Complete

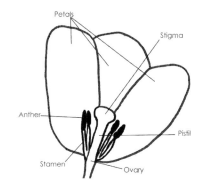

1. Read the following introduction to your students:

   Remember earlier we looked at a flower and talked about what it does? Now, we are going to take a flower apart!

2. Give each student a tulip bloom to examine. Use the diagram above to help point out the parts of the flower as they observe the bloom. Begin by pointing out the petals of the flower, and explain that these are there to help attract insects to the flower.

3. {**Adults Only**} Next, point out the anthers and the pollen on them. Share with the students that these are known as the male parts of a flower. Cut one of the anthers, and use the magnifying glass to look at the pollen. (Note—*Be careful with the pollen because it can stain clothing*).

4. Then, point out the pistil in the center, and share that these are the female parts of a flower. Use a Q-tip to show how a pollinator transfers the pollen to the top of the pistil.

5. {**Adults Only**} Cut out the pistil and split it in half so that your students can observe the inside.

6. Allow your students time to make additional observations.

Explanation

The point of this demonstration was to give the students a chance to observe all the parts of a flower.

Nature Study: Flowers

This week, you will look at the different flowers in your neighborhood.

Preparation

↻ Read pp. 456-457 in the *Handbook of Nature Study* to learn more about flowers and their purpose.

Outdoor Time

☼ Go on a walk and observe the different types of flowers around the path. Allow the students to observe the flowers, look for the parts they know, and ask any questions they may have. You can use the information you have learned from reading the *Handbook of Nature Study* to answer their questions or to share information about what they are observing.

Coordinating Activities

✂ **Art** – (Field of Flowers) Have the students paint a field of flowers on a sheet of paper. Let the students' imaginations run free for this project. The results will be beautiful and interesting!

✂ **Snack** – (Flower Cake) Have a piece of cake that is decorated with icing flowers.

✂ **Activity** – (Nature Prints) Have the students use several flowers to make a print. You will need a large, white T-shirt, cardboard, flowers, tape, newspaper, towels, and a hammer. You can find the directions for this project at the following website:

🖱 https://elementalscience.com/blogs/science-activities/nature-print-t-shirt

Note—*Set the T-shirt aside because the students will have the option to add to it in week 4.*

Write – Simple Notebooking

Student Diary

☐ **Main Idea Page** – Have the students color the coloring page found on SD p. 117.

☐ **Demonstration Sheet** – After you do the demonstration, fill out the demonstration sheet found on SD p. 118 with the students.

☐ **Nature Journal Sheet** – After you have your nature study time, fill out the nature journal sheet found on SD p. 119 with the students. The students can sketch what they have seen, or you can write down their observations.

☐ **Art Page** – Have the students use SD p. 120 to complete the art activity.

Lapbooking Templates

📁 **Weekly Mini-book** – Have the students cut out and color the Flowers Mini-book on LT p. 50. You can have them cut out the main idea graphic included and glue it in the interior of the mini-book, or you can write a sentence with what they have learned from the week for them on the inside of the mini-book. Once the students are done, have them glue the booklet into the mini-lapbook.

📁 **Overall Lapbook** – Have the students add the page they painted to the "My Botany Projects" pocket in the lapbook.

Week 3: Seeds

2-Days-a-Week Schedule

	Day 1	Day 2
Read	❑ Read the introduction with the students ❑ Read the selected pages in *The Usborne Children's Encyclopedia*	❑ Choose one or more of the additional books to read from this week
Do	❑ Complete the Scientific Demonstration "Always Up" ❑ Eat "Edible Seeds" for snack	❑ Complete the Nature Study "Seeds" ❑ Do the "Seed Prints" activity
Write	❑ Color the main idea page ❑ Fill out the demonstration sheet	❑ Fill out the nature journal sheet ❑ Complete the art page

5-Days-a-Week Schedule

	Day 1	Day 2	Day 3	Day 4	Day 5
Read	❑ Read the introduction with the students	❑ Read the selected pages in *The Usborne Children's Encyclopedia*	❑ Choose one or more of the additional books to read from this week	❑ Choose one or more of the additional books to read from this week	
Do	❑ Eat "Edible Seeds" for snack	❑ Complete the Scientific Demonstration "Always Up"	❑ Work on the activity "Seed Collage"	❑ Do the "Seed Prints" activity	❑ Complete the Nature Study "Seeds"
Write	❑ Color the main idea page	❑ Fill out the demonstration sheet	❑ Complete the Seeds Mini-book	❑ Complete the art page	❑ Fill out the nature journal sheet

Read – Information Gathering

Weekly Topic

🌱 Seeds contain tiny baby plants.

Scripted Introduction

(Note—You will need to soak a bean seed overnight for this week's introduction.)

Have a lima bean seed that has been soaked overnight out on a plate on the table in front of you. Say to the students:

> Last week we looked at flowers and how they have the parts of a plant that are needed to make a seed. This week, we are going to look closer at the seeds.

As you describe the different parts of the seed, point to them on the lima bean or on the sheet from the appendix on p. 196.

> A seed contains a baby plant in it. On the outside of the seed is the seed coat, which protects what is inside. Most of what is inside the seed is a food store for the baby plant, but at the top, there is the beginning of the plant, which starts at the radicle.
>
> The little offshoot includes the epicotyl and hypocotyl. These parts develop into the roots and the stem with leaves when conditions are right. This week, we are going to take a closer look at seeds.

Read–Alouds

Encyclopedia Pages

📖 *The Usborne Children's Encyclopedia* pp. 94-95 "How Plants Grow"

Library Books to Look For

📖 *The Magic School Bus Plants Seeds: A Book About How Living Things Grow* by Joanna Cole
📖 *Seeds* by Ken Robbins
📖 *A Fruit Is a Suitcase for Seeds* by Jean Richards and Anca Hariton
📖 *Curious George Plants a Seed* (Curious George Early Readers) by H. A. Rey

Do – Hands-on Projects

Scientific Demonstration: Always Up

Materials Needed

✓ 3 Bean seeds

✓ Paper towel
✓ Plastic baggie
✓ Tape
✓ Water

Steps to Complete

1. Read the following introduction to your students:

   Remember earlier we looked at a seed? We are going to watch our seeds sprout and see which way they grow!

2. Dampen a paper towel, fold it, and place it in the bottom of the baggie.

3. Have the students place the three bean seeds at different angles on the paper towel.

4. Seal the baggie up, and tape it to the side of your refrigerator.

5. Check the baggie each day for the next five days. Once the seed sprouts, ask the students:

   ? Which way did the seed grow?

Explanation

Read the following explaination to the students:

We oserved the seeds sprout, each one of them sending the stem and leaves up and the roots down, no matter in which position they begin. Plants do this naturally so that the leaves will be exposed to the sun and the roots can help anchor the plant in the soil.

Nature Study: Seeds

This week, you will look at the different seeds in your neighborhood.

Preparation

◌ Read pp. 458-459 (section on seed germination) in the *Handbook of Nature Study* to learn more about seeds.

Outdoor Time

☼ Go on a walk and collect the various seeds you find. Allow the students to make observations about the different types of seeds and their shapes and sizes. When you return home, plant some of your seeds in eggshells, as described in the *Handbook of Nature Study*. Afterward, have the students make an entry into their nature journal.

Coordinating Activities

✂ Art – (Seed Prints) Have a plate with red paint on it for the students to use. Cut an apple in half horizontally instead of vertically so that the seed pods will create a star pattern.

Have the students dip the apple half in the paint and use it to stamp a design on the paper.

✂ Snack – (Edible Seeds) Explain to the students that we can eat many different types of seeds and that we also eat fruits, which contain seeds. Have several types of fruit and seeds, such as cherry tomatoes, strawberries, blackberries, sunflower seeds, and pumpkin seeds. Enjoy trying the different fruits and seeds as you talk about how they look and taste different.

✂ Activity – (Seeds Collage) Have the students make a seed collage. You will need a paintbrush, paper, glue, and seeds. Have the students paint a picture in glue on a piece of construction paper. Then, use different types of seeds to create a collage out of their pictures.

Write – Simple Notebooking

Student Diary

☐ Main Idea Page – Have the students color the coloring page found on SD p. 121.

☐ Demonstration Sheet – After you do the demonstration, fill out the demonstration sheet found on SD p. 122 with the students.

☐ Nature Journal Sheet – After you have your nature study time, fill out the nature journal sheet found on SD p. 123 with the students. The students can sketch what they have seen, or you can write down their observations.

☐ Art Page – Have the students use SD p. 124 to complete the art activity.

Lapbooking Templates

📁 Weekly Mini-book – Have the students cut out and color the Seeds Mini-book on LT p. 51. You can have them cut out the main idea graphic included and glue it in the interior of the mini-book, or you can write a sentence with what they have learned from the week for them on the inside of the mini-book. Once the students are done, have them glue the booklet into the mini-lapbook.

📁 Overall Lapbook – Have the students add the page they painted to the "My Botany Projects" pocket in the lapbook.

Week 4: Leaves

2-Days-a-Week Schedule		
	Day 1	**Day 2**
Read	❑ Read the introduction with the students ❑ Read the selected pages in *The Usborne Children's Encyclopedia*	❑ Choose one or more of the additional books to read from this week
Do	❑ Complete the Scientific Demonstration "Leaf Cover-up" ❑ Eat "Edible Leaves" for snack	❑ Complete the Nature Study "Leaves" ❑ Do the "Leaf Rubbings" activity
Write	❑ Color the main idea page ❑ Fill out the demonstration sheet	❑ Fill out the nature journal sheet ❑ Complete the art page

5-Days-a-Week Schedule					
	Day 1	**Day 2**	**Day 3**	**Day 4**	**Day 5**
Read	❑ Read the introduction with the students	❑ Read the selected pages in *The Usborne Children's Encyclopedia*	❑ Choose one or more of the additional books to read from this week	❑ Choose one or more of the additional books to read from this week	
Do	❑ Eat "Edible Leaves" for snack	❑ Complete the Scientific Demonstration "Leaf Cover-up"	❑ Work on the activity "Nature Prints, Part 2"	❑ Do the "Leaf Rubbings" activity	❑ Complete the Nature Study "Leaves"
Write	❑ Color the main idea page	❑ Fill out the demonstration sheet	❑ Complete the Leaves Mini-book	❑ Complete the art page	❑ Fill out the nature journal sheet

Read – Information Gathering

Weekly Topic

- Leaves help the plant make food.

Scripted Introduction

Have a bean plant on the table in front of you. Say to the students:

We can see several parts of the bean plant here above the soil.

? Can you name any of those parts?

That's great! We can easily see the stem, flowers, and the leaves. Leaves are the part of the plant that are responsible for making the plant's food.

Leaves have a special pigment in them called chlorophyll, which makes the leaves green. The pigment's job is to take in sunlight and convert it into energy that the plant can use to make food.

This week, we are going to take a closer look at leaves.

You may want to pull a leaf off of the plant and allow the students to observe it up close.

Read–Alouds

Encyclopedia Pages

- *The Usborne Children's Encyclopedia* p. 97 "Leaves"

Library Books to Look For

- *Leaves* (Plant Parts series) by Vijaya Bodach,
- *I Am A Leaf* (Level 1 – Hello Reader) by Jean Marzollo and Judith Moffatt
- *Leaves* by David Ezra Stein

Do – Hands-on Projects

Scientific Demonstration: Leaf Cover-up

Materials Needed

- ✓ Bean plant
- ✓ Paper
- ✓ Paper clip

Steps to Complete

1. Read the following introduction to your students:

   Remember earlier we looked at the different parts of our bean plant? Now, we are going to cover one of the leaves and see if it changes!

2. Have the students choose a leaf on your bean plant.

3. {**Adults Only**} Cut out a 1-inch strip of paper long enough to fold over your leaf so that it covers both sides.

4. Have the students use the paper clip to firmly attach the paper to your leaf so that it covers a portion of the leaf, but not all of it. Then, let the plant sit in the sun for three to four days.

5. After several days take off the piece of paper. Ask the students:

   ? What happened to the leaf that was covered?

   ? How is it different from the leaves that weren't covered?

Explanation

Read the following explaination to the students:

We saw that the leaf that was covered turned a bit yellow. This is because the chlorophyll in the leaf has moved out of that section to a place where it is able to continue to absorb sunlight and make energy for the plant.

Nature Study: Leaves

This week, you will look at the different leaves in your neighborhood.

Preparation

↻ Read pp. 626-627 (section on making leaf prints) in the *Handbook of Nature Study* to learn more about making leaf prints.

Outdoor Time

☼ Go on a walk and collect the leaves you find. Allow the students to make observations about the different types of leaves and their shapes and sizes. When you return home make leaf prints, as described in the *Handbook of Nature Study*, and add them into their nature journal.

Coordinating Activities

✂ **Art** – (Leaf Rubbings) Go outside and collect a few leaves. Once inside have the students lay out a leaf design under piece of paper. Then, have the students rub the side of a crayon over it to make a beautiful leaf rubbing design.

✂ **Snack** – (Edible Leaves) Explain to the students that we can eat many different types of leaves. Have several types of leaves they can eat, such as lettuce, spinach, kale, or bok choy, along with some ranch dressing. Enjoy trying the leaves after dipping them in ranch dressing as you talk about their different looks and tastes.

✂ **Activity** – (Nature Prints, Part 2) Have the students add several leaves to the nature print. You will need the T-shirt from the week 2 activity, leaves, tape, newspaper, towels, and a hammer. You can find the directions for this project at the following website:

🖱 https://elementalscience.com/blogs/science-activities/nature-print-t-shirt

Write – Simple Notebooking

Student Diary

- ☐ **Main Idea Page** – Have the students color the coloring page found on SD p. 125.

- ☐ **Demonstration Sheet** – After you do the demonstration, fill out the demonstration sheet found on SD p. 126 with the students.

- ☐ **Nature Journal Sheet** – After you have your nature study time, fill out the nature journal sheet found on SD p. 127 with the students. The students can sketch what they have seen, or you can write down their observations.

- ☐ **Art Page** – Have the students use SD p. 128 to complete the art activity.

Lapbooking Templates

- 🗁 **Weekly Mini-book** – Have the students cut out and color the Leaves Mini-book on LT p. 52. You can have them cut out the main idea graphic included and glue it in the interior of the mini-book, or you can write a sentence with what they have learned from the week for them on the inside of the mini-book. Once the students are done, have them glue the booklet into the mini-lapbook.

- 🗁 **Overall Lapbook** – Have the students add the page they painted to the "My Botany Projects" pocket in the lapbook.

Week 5: Stems

2-Days-a-Week Schedule		
	Day 1	**Day 2**
Read	❑ Read the introduction with the students ❑ Read the selected pages in *The Usborne Children's Encyclopedia*	❑ Choose one or more of the additional books to read from this week
Do	❑ Complete the Scientific Demonstration "Thirsty Stems" ❑ Eat "Edible Stems" for snack	❑ Complete the Nature Study "Oak Tree" ❑ Do the "Blowing Stems" activity
Write	❑ Color the main idea page ❑ Fill out the demonstration sheet	❑ Fill out the nature journal sheet ❑ Complete the art page

5-Days-a-Week Schedule					
	Day 1	**Day 2**	**Day 3**	**Day 4**	**Day 5**
Read	❑ Read the introduction with the students	❑ Read the selected pages in *The Usborne Children's Encyclopedia*	❑ Choose one or more of the additional books to read from this week	❑ Choose one or more of the additional books to read from this week	
Do	❑ Eat "Edible Stems" for snack	❑ Complete the Scientific Demonstration "Thirsty Stems"	❑ Work on the activity "Bark Rubbings"	❑ Do the "Blowing Stems" activity	❑ Complete the Nature Study "Oak Tree"
Write	❑ Color the main idea page	❑ Fill out the demonstration sheet	❑ Complete the Stems Mini-book	❑ Complete the art page	❑ Fill out the nature journal sheet

Read – Information Gathering

Weekly Topic

🌱 The stem of a plant acts as its highway.

Scripted Introduction

Have a piece of celery and a magnifying glass out on the table in front of you. Say to the students:

> This piece of celery is actually the stem of a plant. Let's take a closer look using this magnifying glass.
>
> **?** Do you see the tubes running up the side of the piece of celery?
>
> The job of these tubes is to carry water and nutrients up the plant and food down the plant. In other words, the stem acts as the highway of the plant, moving things around to where they need to be quickly.
>
> This week, we are going to spend some more time looking at stems.

Allow the students to have some more time to look at the piece of celery with their magnifying glasses.

Read-Alouds

Encyclopedia Pages

📖 *The Usborne Children's Encyclopedia* – There are no new pages scheduled.

Library Books to Look For

📖 *Stems* (Plant Parts) by Vijaya Bodach
📖 *Plant Stems & Roots* (Look Once, Look Again Science Series) by David M. Schwartz
📖 *Stems* (First Step Nonfiction) by Melanie Mitchell

Do – Hands-on Projects

Scientific Demonstration: Thirsty Stems

Materials Needed

✓ Celery (with leaves)
✓ Food coloring
✓ Glass and water

Steps to Complete

1. Read the following introduction to your students:

    Remember earlier we looked closer at a stem of celery? We saw tubes running up the sides. This week, we are going to see exactly what those tubes do for a plant!

2. Add several drops of food coloring to the water in a glass.

3. Place your piece of celery in the glass, and set it aside for three days.

4. After several days, observe what has happened to the piece of celery and ask the students:

    ? What happened to the celery?

Explanation

Read the following explaination to the students:

We saw the celery slowly turn the color of the water that it was in. As the water was transported up through the stem, the food coloring was also transported with it. This is the same way that nutrients are transported through a plant.

Nature Study: Oak Tree

This week, you are studying stems, which is a great time to look at trees because the trunk and branches of a tree are really giant stems. This week, your focus will be on oak trees.

Preparation

↷ Read pp. 638-642 in the *Handbook of Nature Study* to learn more about oak trees.

Outdoor Time

☼ Go on a walk and look for oak trees. Allow the students to observe the tree and ask any questions they may have. You can use the information you have learned from reading the *Handbook of Nature Study* to answer their questions or to share information about what they are observing.

Coordinating Activities

✂ **Art** – (Blowing Stems) Mix a little brown or green paint with some water to dilute the paint a bit. Place a large drop of the watered-down paint at the bottom of a sheet of paper. Then, have the students use a straw to blow the drop of paint into stems. Allow it to dry before adding leaves and flowers to the plants.

✂ **Snack** – (Edible Stems) Explain that celery is a stem we can eat! Serve celery sticks filled with cream cheese for snack.

✂ **Activity** – (Bark Rubbings) Have the students examine bark, which covers the "stem" of a tree. You will need paper and crayons. Head outside with the students to find several different kinds of trees to use for bark samples. After you have selected a tree, have the students place a piece of paper on the tree trunk and rub on the top with a crayon until the shape of the bark appears. Repeat the process with several different types of trees. (Note— *The students should see a variety of patterns in the bark from different trees.*)

Write – Simple Notebooking

Student Diary

- ☐ Main Idea Page – Have the students color the coloring page found on SD p. 129.
- ☐ Demonstration Sheet – After you do the demonstration, fill out the demonstration sheet found on SD p. 130 with the students.
- ☐ Nature Journal Sheet – After you have your nature study time, fill out the nature journal sheet found on SD p. 131 with the students. The students can sketch what they have seen, or you can write down their observations.
- ☐ Art Page – Have the students use SD p. 132 to complete the art activity.

Lapbooking Templates

- ☐ Weekly Mini-book – Have the students cut out and color the Stem Mini-book on LT p. 53. You can have them cut out the main idea graphic included and glue it in the interior of the mini-book, or you can write a sentence with what they have learned from the week for them on the inside of the mini-book. Once the students are done, have them glue the booklet into the mini-lapbook.
- ☐ Overall Lapbook – Have the students add the page they painted to the "My Botany Projects" pocket in the lapbook.

Week 6: Roots

2-Days-a-Week Schedule		
	Day 1	**Day 2**
Read	❑ Read the introduction with the students ❑ Read the selected pages in *The Usborne Children's Encyclopedia*	❑ Choose one or more of the additional books to read from this week
Do	❑ Complete the Scientific Demonstration "Growing Roots" ❑ Eat "Edible Roots" for snack	❑ Complete the Nature Study "Maple Tree" ❑ Do the "Painting with Roots" activity
Write	❑ Color the main idea page ❑ Fill out the demonstration sheet	❑ Fill out the nature journal sheet ❑ Complete the art page

5-Days-a-Week Schedule					
	Day 1	**Day 2**	**Day 3**	**Day 4**	**Day 5**
Read	❑ Read the introduction with the students	❑ Read the selected pages in *The Usborne Children's Encyclopedia*	❑ Choose one or more of the additional books to read from this week	❑ Choose one or more of the additional books to read from this week	
Do	❑ Eat "Edible Roots" for snack	❑ Complete the Scientific Demonstration "Growing Roots"	❑ Go on a field trip to a Greenhouse	❑ Do the "Painting with Roots" activity	❑ Complete the Nature Study "Maple Tree"
Write	❑ Color the main idea page	❑ Fill out the demonstration sheet	❑ Complete the Roots Mini-book	❑ Complete the art page	❑ Fill out the nature journal sheet

Read – Information Gathering

Weekly Topic

❧ Roots take in water and nutrients from the soil.

Scripted Introduction

Have a green onion, complete with roots, out on the table in front of you. Say to the students:

> This green onion still has its roots on it.

Point out the roots to the students, and allow them to observe the roots for a moment before continuing.

> Normally, the roots of a plant are underground. This is because their job is to absorb water and nutrients from the soil. The plant then transports these ingredients through the stems and into the leaves to make food for the plant.

> This week, we are going to take a closer look at roots.

You may also want to dig up the bean plant you planted earlier in this unit to examine its roots.

Read–Alouds

Encyclopedia Pages

📖 *The Usborne Children's Encyclopedia* – There are no new pages scheduled.

Library Books to Look For

📖 *Roots* (First Step Nonfiction) by Melanie Mitchell
📖 *Roots* (Plant Parts series) by Vijaya Bodach
📖 *Plant Plumbing: A Book About Roots and Stems* by Susan Blackaby

Do – Hands-on Projects

Scientific Demonstration: Growing Roots

Materials Needed

✓ Green onion
✓ Cup
✓ Water

Steps to Complete

1. Read the following introduction to your students:

Remember earlier we looked at the roots of a green onion? Over this week, we are going to watch how those roots grow!

2. {**Adults Only**} Trim most of the roots off the bottom of the green onion. Be sure to leave all off the white part of the bottom. Only trim off the majority of the "stringy" parts.

3. Have the students fill the cup halfway with water, and put the stems in water.

4. Then, wait several days for the roots to grow. It can take anywhere from two to seven days, so keep checking each day and be patient.

5. Once the roots begin to grow, take the onion out of the water, and let the students observe them. Ask the students:

   ? Do these roots look the same as the ones we saw at the beginning of the week?

Explanation

Read the following explaination to the students:

We saw roots grow over the week from the green onion. If we left it in the water, the roots would continue to grow. We could also stick the green onion in soil. If we kept watering it, the green onion would continue to grow.

Nature Study: Maple Tree

This week, you are studying roots. Because roots are hard to study without digging up lots of plants, you will study another type of tree this week.

Preparation

⟳ Read pp. 628-633 in the *Handbook of Nature Study* to learn more about maple trees.

Outdoor Time

☼ Go on a walk and look for maple trees. Allow the students to observe the tree and ask any questions they may have. You can use the information you have learned from reading the *Handbook of Nature Study* to answer their questions or to share information about what they are observing.

Coordinating Activities

✂ Art – (Painting with Roots) Use the green onion you examined in the introduction as a paintbrush. Allow the students to create their own masterpiece using their root brush!

✂ Snack – (Edible Roots) Explain that we eat several different types of roots. These include potatoes, carrots, radishes, and other root vegetables. Serve carrot sticks or shoestring potato sticks for snack.

✂ Activity – (Greenhouse) Wrap up your plant studies by taking a field trip to a greenhouse.

While you are there, look for the different parts of the plant that you have learned about during this botany unit.

Write – Simple Notebooking

Student Diary

- [ ] **Main Idea Page** – Have the students color the coloring page found on SD p. 133.
- [ ] **Demonstration Sheet** – After you do the demonstration, fill out the demonstration sheet found on SD p. 134 with the students.
- [ ] **Nature Journal Sheet** – After you have your nature study time, fill out the nature journal sheet found on SD p. 135 with the students. The students can sketch what they have seen, or you can write down their observations.
- [ ] **Art Page** – Have the students use SD p. 136 to complete the art activity.

Lapbooking Templates

- [ ] **Weekly Mini-book** – Have the students cut out and color the Roots Mini-book on LT p. 54. You can have them cut out the main idea graphic included and glue it in the interior of the mini-book, or you can write a sentence with what they have learned from the week for them on the inside of the mini-book. Once the students are done, have them glue the booklet into the mini-lapbook.
- [ ] **Overall Lapbook** – Have the students add the page they painted to the "My Botany Projects" pocket in the lapbook.

Intro to Science

Unit 6: Intro to Zoology

Intro to Zoology Unit Overview

Sequence for Study

- 🐾 **Week 1:** Mammals
- 🐾 **Week 2:** Reptiles
- 🐾 **Week 3:** Birds
- 🐾 **Week 4:** Butterflies
- 🐾 **Week 5:** Invertebrates
- 🐾 **Week 6:** Fish

Supplies Needed for the Unit

Week	Introduction Props	Hands-on Project Materials	Coordinating Activities Supplies
1	Pictures of mammals	Three pictures of mammals	Animal crackers, Mammal pictures from old magazines or animal stickers
2	Pictures of reptiles	Thermometer	Peanut butter, Powdered milk, Honey, Cocoa, Vanilla, Chopped Nuts, Raisins, Mini M&M's, Pictures of reptiles, 2 Colors of paint, Paper, Black Marker
3	Pictures of birds	Cheerios, Pipe cleaner	Mangoes, blueberries, or strawberries, Sunflower seeds, Pipe cleaners, Feathers, Paint, Paper
4	Pictures of butterflies	Butterfly life cycle cards from appendix	Lettuce, Eyedropper, Paint, Paper, Glitter, Sequins, Glue, Butterfly outline on paper
5	Pictures of invertebrates	Plate, Several types of food (i.e., bread, cheese, crackers, honey, and fruit)	Gummy worms, 1 Large and 1 small Styrofoam balls, Black paint, Googly eyes, Black pipe cleaners, Paint, Thick string, Paper
6	Pictures of fish	*No supplies needed.*	Goldfish crackers, Paper, Watercolor paints, Glitter, Construction paper, Paper clips, Magnet, Dowel rod, String

Books Scheduled

Hands-on Projects

📖 *Handbook of Nature Study (If you are using the nature study option.)*

Scheduled Encylopedias

📖 *The Usborne Children's Encyclopedia*

Library Books to Look For

Week 1
📖 *About Mammals: A Guide For Children* by Cathryn Sill and John Sill
📖 *Eye Wonder: Mammals* (Eye Wonder) by Sarah Walker
📖 *Is a Camel a Mammal?* by Tish Rabe and Jim Durk
📖 *Animals Called Mammals* (What Kind of Animal Is It?) by Bobbie Kalman

Week 2
📖 *Miles and Miles of Reptiles: All About Reptiles* by Tish Rabe and Aristides Ruiz
📖 *Eye Wonder: Reptiles* (Eye Wonder) by Simon Holland
📖 *Reptiles* (True Books : Animals) by Melissa Stewart
📖 *Fun Facts About Snakes!* (I Like Reptiles and Amphibians!) by Carmen Bredeson

Week 3
📖 *About Birds: A Guide for Children* by Cathryn Sill and John Sill
📖 *Fine Feathered Friends: All About Birds* by Tish Rabe
📖 *How Do Birds Find Their Way?* (Let's-Read-and-Find... Science 2) by Roma Gans
📖 *The Magic School Bus Flies from the Nest* by Joanna Cole and Carolyn Bracken

Week 4
📖 *Butterfly House* by Eve Bunting and Greg Shed
📖 *A Butterfly Grows* (Green Light Readers Level 2) by Stephen R. Swinburne
📖 *From Caterpillar to Butterfly: Following the Life Cycle* by Suzanne Slade
📖 *The Life of a Butterfly* by Clare Hibbert

Week 5
📖 *No Backbone! the World of Invertebrates* by Natalie Lunis
📖 *I Wonder What It's Like to Be an Earthworm* (Hovanec, Erin M. Life Science Wonder Series.) by Erin M. Hovanec
📖 *Are You a Snail?* (Backyard Books) by Judy Allen

Week 6
📖 *What's It Like to Be a Fish?* (Let's-Read-and-Find... Science 1) by Wendy Pfeffer
📖 *Rainbow Fish Big Book* by Marcus Pfister Herbert and J. Alison James
📖 *Fish Eyes: A Book You Can Count On* by Lois Ehlert

Week 1: Mammals

You do not need to complete all of this in a week. Instead, choose from the following options.

2-Days-a-Week Schedule		
	Day 1	**Day 2**
Read	❑ Read the introduction with the students ❑ Read the selected pages in *The Usborne Children's Encyclopedia*	❑ Choose one or more of the additional books to read from this week
Do	❑ Complete the Scientific Demonstration "Comparing Mammals" ❑ Eat "Animal Crackers" for snack	❑ Complete the Nature Study "Rabbits" ❑ Do the "Mammal Collage" activity
Write	❑ Color the main idea page ❑ Fill out the demonstration sheet	❑ Fill out the nature journal sheet ❑ Complete the art page

5-Days-a-Week Schedule					
	Day 1	**Day 2**	**Day 3**	**Day 4**	**Day 5**
Read	❑ Read the introduction with the students	❑ Read the selected pages in *The Usborne Children's Encyclopedia*	❑ Choose one or more of the additional books to read from this week	❑ Choose one or more of the additional books to read from this week	
Do	❑ Eat "Animal Crackers" for snack	❑ Complete the Scientific Demonstration "Comparing Mammals"	❑ Work on the activity "Mammal Classification"	❑ Do the "Mammal Collage" activity	❑ Complete the Nature Study "Rabbits"
Write	❑ Color the main idea page	❑ Fill out the demonstration sheet	❑ Complete the Mammals Mini-book	❑ Complete the art page	❑ Fill out the nature journal sheet

Read – Information Gathering

Weekly Topic

- Mammals, like rabbits, have fur or hair.

Scripted Introduction

Have pictures of mammals out on the table in front of you. Say to the students:

> Mammals are animals that have fur or hair. These animals also feed their young with milk. Did you know that we are mammals?
>
> **?** Can you think of some other mammals?

Let the students share their ideas. *(If the students are unsure, have them look at the pictures you have of mammals and name those.)* Then say:

> Those are great ideas!
>
> Rabbits are also mammals. They have fur, and they feed their babies milk. They are also warm-blooded, which means that they can make their own heat to keep their bodies warm.
>
> This week, we are going to look at different types of mammals and learn more about how they compare to us.

Read–Alouds

Encyclopedia Pages

- *The Usborne Children's Encyclopedia* pp. 60-61 "Mammals"

Library Books to Look For

- *About Mammals: A Guide For Children* by Cathryn Sill and John Sill
- *Eye Wonder: Mammals* (Eye Wonder) by Sarah Walker
- *Is a Camel a Mammal?* by Tish Rabe and Jim Durk
- *Animals Called Mammals* (What Kind of Animal Is It?) by Bobbie Kalman and Kristina Lundblad

Do – Hands-on Projects

Scientific Demonstration: Comparing Mammals

Materials Needed

- ✓ Three pictures of mammals (such as a lion, gorilla, and a rabbit)

Steps to Complete

1. Read the following introduction to your students:

    Remember earlier we looked at several pictures of mammals? Today, we are going to look at more mammal pictures and ask a series of questions about each.

2. Have the students examine each picture, and ask them the following questions:

    ? What do we call this animal?

    ? How big is the animal?

    ? Does the animal have hair? Where is that hair? What does the hair look like?

    ? What does the animal's ear look like?

    ? What kind of teeth does the animal have? Are they sharp or dull? Big or small?

    ? Do you know what the animal eats?

(Note—As they answer the questions, write the students' answers on the demonstration sheet.)

Explanation

The results of this demonstration will vary based on the pictures you chose for the students to examine.

Nature Study: Rabbits

This week, you will look for rabbits in your backyard or park. Be sure to also point out any other mammals you run across, such as squirrels, dogs, and cats.

Preparation

↻ Read pp. 214-218 in the *Handbook of Nature Study* to learn more about mammals and rabbits.

Outdoor Time

☼ Go on a walk and look for rabbits or other mammals to observe. Allow the students to observe them and ask any questions they may have. You can use the information you have learned from reading the *Handbook of Nature Study* to answer their questions or to share information about what they are observing.

Coordinating Activities

✂ Art – (Mammal Collage) Have the students cut out pictures of mammals from old magazines, or use animal stickers that you have purchased. Have them make a collage of mammals on a sheet of paper.

✂ Snack – (Animal Crackers) Have animal crackers for snack one day. Talk about the different kinds of animals you find, what kind of hair, teeth, hands, and noses they have. Also discuss what they eat. (Note—*You could also introduce the concept of herbivores, which eat plants, omnivores, which eat both plants and meat, and carnivores, which eat meat.*)

✂ Activity – (Mammal Classification) Collect pictures of various types of mammals. Have the students separate them into categories that they choose. Some possibilities are to sort by color, by teeth, by where they live, or by what they eat.

Write – Simple Notebooking

Student Diary
- ☐ Main Idea Page – Have the students color the coloring page found on SD p. 139.
- ☐ Demonstration Sheet – As you do the demonstration, fill out the chart on the demonstration sheet found on SD p. 140 with the students.
- ☐ Nature Journal Sheet – After you have your nature study time, fill out the nature journal sheet found on SD p. 141 with the students. The students can sketch what they have seen, or you can write down their observations.
- ☐ Art Page – Have the students use SD p. 142 to complete the art activity.

Lapbooking Templates
- 🗁 Weekly Mini-book – Have the students cut out and color the Mammals Mini-book on LT p. 59. You can have them cut out the main idea graphic included and glue it in the interior of the mini-book, or you can write a sentence with what they have learned from the week for them on the inside of the mini-book. Once the students are done, have them glue the booklet into the mini-lapbook.
- 🗁 Overall Lapbook – Have the students cut out the "My Zoology Projects" pocket on LT p. 65. Have them glue the pocket into the lapbook and add the coloring project they did to the pocket.

Week 2: Reptiles

2-Days-a-Week Schedule		
	Day 1	**Day 2**
Read	❑ Read the introduction with the students ❑ Read the selected pages in *The Usborne Children's Encyclopedia*	❑ Choose one or more of the additional books to read from this week
Do	❑ Complete the Scientific Demonstration "Cold-Blooded" ❑ Eat "Chocolate Snakes" for snack	❑ Complete the Nature Study "Reptiles" ❑ Do the "Fingerprint Snakes" activity
Write	❑ Color the main idea page ❑ Fill out the demonstration sheet	❑ Fill out the nature journal sheet ❑ Complete the art page

5-Days-a-Week Schedule					
	Day 1	**Day 2**	**Day 3**	**Day 4**	**Day 5**
Read	❑ Read the introduction with the students	❑ Read the selected pages in *The Usborne Children's Encyclopedia*	❑ Choose one or more of the additional books to read from this week	❑ Choose one or more of the additional books to read from this week	
Do	❑ Eat "Chocolate Snakes" for snack	❑ Complete the Scientific Demonstration "Cold-Blooded"	❑ Work on the activity "Reptile Classification"	❑ Do the "Fingerprint Snakes" activity	❑ Complete the Nature Study "Reptiles"
Write	❑ Color the main idea page	❑ Fill out the demonstration sheet	❑ Complete the Reptiles Mini-book	❑ Complete the art page	❑ Fill out the nature journal sheet

Read – Information Gathering

Weekly Topic

- Reptiles, like snakes, are cold-blooded.

Scripted Introduction

Have pictures of reptiles out on the table in front of you. Say to the students:

Reptiles, like snakes, are cold-blooded animals, just like fish.

? Do you remember what it means to be cold-blooded?

That's right! Cold-blooded animals take on the temperature of their surroundings because they don't make their own heat. This means that they are hot when their surroundings are hot and cold when their surroundings are cold. All reptiles, including snakes, are cold-blooded.

This week, we are going to look at reptiles.

Read-Alouds

Encyclopedia Pages

- *The Usborne Children's Encyclopedia* pp. 70-71 "Reptile Life"

Library Books to Look For

- *Miles and Miles of Reptiles: All About Reptiles* by Tish Rabe and Aristides Ruiz
- *Eye Wonder: Reptiles* (Eye Wonder) by Simon Holland
- *Reptiles* (True Books : Animals) by Melissa Stewart
- *Fun Facts About Snakes!* (I Like Reptiles and Amphibians!) by Carmen Bredeson

Do – Hands-on Projects

Scientific Demonstration: Cold-Blooded

Materials Needed

- ✓ Thermometer

Steps to Complete

1. Read the following introduction to your students:

   Remember earlier we looked at pictures of reptiles? We learned that reptiles are cold-blooded. Today, we are going to see how these animals control their temperature!

2. Place the thermometer in the sun. Read the thermometer after two minutes. (*The temperature should have increased rapidly.*)

3. Then, place the thermometer in the shade. Read the thermometer after two minutes. (*The temperature should have dropped significantly.*)

Explanation

Read the following explaination to the students:

When the thermometer was in the sun, it heated up quickly. When the thermometer was moved into the shade, the temperature dropped. Reptiles move from areas of shade to cool off and sun to heat up.

Nature Study: Reptiles

This week, you will look for reptiles, such as lizards, in your backyard or park. (If you do find snakes, do not handle them!)

Preparation

↻ Read pp. 193-194 in the *Handbook of Nature Study* to learn more about reptiles. You may want to skim the remaining sections to learn more about specific reptiles in your area.

Outdoor Time

☼ Go on a walk and look for reptiles (such as lizards) to observe. Allow the students to observe them and ask any questions they may have. You can use the information you have learned from reading the *Handbook of Nature Study* to answer their questions or to share information about what they are observing.

Coordinating Activities

✂ **Art** – (Fingerprint Snake) See this website for directions:

🖱 http://www.dltk-kids.com/crafts/miscellaneous/fingerprint_snake.htm

✂ **Snack** – (Chocolate Snakes) You will need ½ cup peanut butter, ½ cup powdered milk, ½ cup honey, 1 tbsp cocoa, ½ tsp vanilla, ½ cup chopped nuts, ½ cup raisins, and mini M&M's. (**Note**—*If the students are allergic to peanuts, substitute another nut butter.*) Combine the peanut butter and the powdered milk until blended. Stir in honey, cocoa, vanilla, nuts, and raisins – in that order. Roll your mixture into small snake shapes, and add two mini M&M's for eyes using peanut butter to attach the candies. Place the snakes on wax paper on a cookie sheet, and chill in the refrigerator until firm.

✂ **Activity** – (Reptile Classification) Collect pictures of various types of reptiles. Have the students separate them into categories that they choose. Some possibilities are to sort by color, by where they live, or by what they eat.

Write – Simple Notebooking

Student Diary

- ☐ **Main Idea Page** – Have the students color the coloring page found on SD p. 143.
- ☐ **Demonstration Sheet** – After you do the demonstration, fill out the demonstration sheet found on SD p. 144 with the students.
- ☐ **Nature Journal Sheet** – After you have your nature study time, fill out the nature journal sheet found on SD p. 145 with the students. The students can sketch what they have seen, or you can write down their observations.
- ☐ **Art Page** – Have the students use SD p. 146 to complete the art activity.

Lapbooking Templates

- 📁 **Weekly Mini-book** – Have the students cut out and color the Reptiles Mini-book on LT p. 60. You can have them cut out the main idea graphic included and glue it in the interior of the mini-book, or you can write a sentence with what they have learned from the week for them on the inside of the mini-book. Once the students are done, have them glue the booklet into the mini-lapbook.
- 📁 **Overall Lapbook** – Have the students add the page they painted to the "My Zoology Projects" pocket in the lapbook.

Week 3: Birds

2-Days-a-Week Schedule		
	Day 1	**Day 2**
Read	❑ Read the introduction with the students ❑ Read the selected pages in *The Usborne Children's Encyclopedia*	❑ Choose one or more of the additional books to read from this week
Do	❑ Complete the Scientific Demonstration "Cereal Feeder" ❑ Eat "Like a Bird" for snack	❑ Complete the Nature Study "Birds" ❑ Do the "Feather Painting" activity
Write	❑ Color the main idea page ❑ Fill out the demonstration sheet	❑ Fill out the nature journal sheet ❑ Complete the art page

5-Days-a-Week Schedule					
	Day 1	**Day 2**	**Day 3**	**Day 4**	**Day 5**
Read	❑ Read the introduction with the students	❑ Read the selected pages in *The Usborne Children's Encyclopedia*	❑ Choose one or more of the additional books to read from this week	❑ Choose one or more of the additional books to read from this week	
Do	❑ Eat "Like a Bird" for snack	❑ Complete the Scientific Demonstration "Cereal Feeder"	❑ Work on the activity "Eating Worms"	❑ Do the "Feather Painting" activity	❑ Complete the Nature Study "Birds"
Write	❑ Color the main idea page	❑ Fill out the demonstration sheet	❑ Complete the Birds Mini-book	❑ Complete the art page	❑ Fill out the nature journal sheet

Read – Information Gathering

Weekly Topic

- Birds have wings and feathers.

Scripted Introduction

Have pictures of birds out on the table in front of you. Say to the students:

? What do you notice about all these animals?

Give the students time to answer before saying:

Those are some good observations! All of these animals are birds. They have wings and feathers that help them fly.

This week, we are going to look at birds.

Read–Alouds

Encyclopedia Pages

📖 *The Usborne Children's Encyclopedia* pp. 64-65 "Bird Life"

Library Books to Look For

📖 *About Birds: A Guide for Children* by Cathryn Sill and John Sill
📖 *Fine Feathered Friends: All About Birds* by Tish Rabe
📖 *How Do Birds Find Their Way?* (Let's-Read-and-Find Out Science 2) by Roma Gans
📖 *The Magic School Bus Flies from the Nest* by Joanna Cole and Carolyn Bracken

Do – Hands-on Projects

Scientific Demonstration: Cereal Feeder

Materials Needed

- ✓ Cheerios
- ✓ Pipe cleaner

Steps to Complete

1. Read the following introduction to your students:

Remember earlier we looked at several pictures of birds? Now we are going to make a bird feeder out of cereal to attract some live birds to our backyard!

2. Give the students a pipe cleaner and a bowl full of Cheerios. Have them string the Cheerios onto the pipe cleaner.

3. Then, have the students shape the pipe cleaner into a ring and twist it together.

4. When they are done, head outside and hang their Cheerio bird feeder ring on a nearby branch, one that is visible from one of your windows.

5. Head back inside with the students, and watch the feeder for the next thirty minutes, recording any visitors on the demonstration sheet.

Explanation

The students should be able to observe several different types of birds coming to eat at the bird feeder.

Nature Study: Birds

This week, you will spend more time looking for the birds in your area.

Preparation

↻ Read pp. 27-43 in the *Handbook of Nature Study* to learn more about birds.

Outdoor Time

☼ Go on a walk and look for birds to observe. Allow the students to observe them and ask any questions they may have. You can use the information you have learned from reading the *Handbook of Nature Study* to answer their questions or to share information about what they are observing.

Coordinating Activities

✂ **Art** – (Feather Painting) Collect feathers from outside, or buy feathers from the store. Give the students a sheet of paper and some paint. Have them use the feathers as paintbrushes to paint a picture.

✂ **Snack** – (Like a Bird) Explain to the students that many birds eat fruit and seeds. Serve various types of fruits, such as mangoes, blueberries, or strawberries, along with a few sunflower seeds for snack.

✂ **Activity** – (Eating Worms) Cut up several pipe cleaners into worm-sized pieces. Give each of the students a clothespin and tell them that this is their beak. Then, have them collect as many worms as they can with their beaks!

Write – Simple Notebooking

Student Diary

- ☐ Main Idea Page – Have the students color the coloring page found on SD p. 147.

- ☐ Demonstration Sheet – After you do the demonstration, fill out the demonstration sheet found on SD p. 148 with the students.

- ☐ Nature Journal Sheet – After you have your nature study time, fill out the nature journal sheet found on SD p. 149 with the students. The students can sketch what they have seen, or you can write down their observations.

- ☐ Art Page – Have the students use SD p. 150 to complete the art activity.

Lapbooking Templates

- ☐ Weekly Mini-book – Have the students cut out and color the Birds Mini-book on LT p. 61. You can have them cut out the main idea graphic included and glue it in the interior of the mini-book, or you can write a sentence with what they have learned from the week for them on the inside of the mini-book. Once the students are done, have them glue the booklet into the mini-lapbook.

- ☐ Overall Lapbook – Have the students add the page they painted to the "My Zoology Projects" pocket in the lapbook.

Week 4: Butterflies

2-Days-a-Week Schedule		
	Day 1	**Day 2**
Read	❑ Read the introduction with the students ❑ Read the selected pages in *The Usborne Children's Encyclopedia*	❑ Choose one or more of the additional books to read from this week
Do	❑ Complete the Scientific Demonstration "Butterfly Life Cycle" ❑ Eat "Like a Caterpillar" for snack	❑ Complete the Nature Study "Butterflies" ❑ Do the "Butterfly Beauty" activity
Write	❑ Color the main idea page ❑ Fill out the demonstration sheet	❑ Fill out the nature journal sheet ❑ Complete the art page

5-Days-a-Week Schedule					
	Day 1	**Day 2**	**Day 3**	**Day 4**	**Day 5**
Read	❑ Read the introduction with the students	❑ Read the selected pages in *The Usborne Children's Encyclopedia*	❑ Choose one or more of the additional books to read from this week	❑ Choose one or more of the additional books to read from this week	
Do	❑ Eat "Like a Caterpillar" for snack	❑ Complete the Scientific Demonstration "Butterfly Life Cycle"	❑ Work on the activity "Butterfly Symmetry"	❑ Do the "Butterfly Beauty" activity	❑ Complete the Nature Study "Butterflies"
Write	❑ Color the main idea page	❑ Fill out the demonstration sheet	❑ Complete the Butterfly Mini-book	❑ Complete the art page	❑ Fill out the nature journal sheet

Read – Information Gathering

Weekly Topic

↳ Caterpillars make a chrysalis and then come out as a butterfly.

Scripted Introduction

Have pictures of butterflies out on the table in front of you. Say to the students:

? What do you notice about all these animals?

Give the students time to answer before saying:

Those are some good observations! All of these animals are butterflies. Butterflies go through a major change during their lifetime called a life cycle.

They hatch from eggs as caterpillars. After some time, these caterpillars make a chrysalis. Then, after some more time, the animals emerge as butterflies.

After the cycle is complete the mature butterflies go and lay more eggs to begin the cycle again.

This week, we are going to look at butterflies.

Read–Alouds

Encyclopedia Pages

▭ *The Usborne Children's Encyclopedia* pp. 76-77 "Butterflies"

Library Books to Look For

▭ *Butterfly House* by Eve Bunting and Greg Shed
▭ *A Butterfly Grows* (Green Light Readers Level 2) by Stephen R. Swinburne
▭ *From Caterpillar to Butterfly: Following the Life Cycle* by Suzanne Slade
▭ *The Life of a Butterfly* by Clare Hibbert

Do – Hands-on Projects

Scientific Demonstration: Butterfly Life Cycle

Materials Needed

✓ Butterfly Life Cycle Cards from appendix p. 197

Steps to Complete

1. Read the following introduction to your students:

   Remember earlier we looked at several picture of butterflies? Now, we are going to look closer at the life cycle of a butterfly!

2. Give the students the butterfly life cycle pictures from appendix p. 197. Have them color the pictures and then cut each one out.

3. Discuss with the students the order of the butterfly's life cycle as they place the pictures in order on the demonstration sheet.

4. Once the students understand the life cycle, have them glue the pictures down.

Nature Study: Butterflies

This week, you will look at the butterflies in your area.

Preparation

↻ Read pp. 301-309 in the *Handbook of Nature Study* to learn more about the black swallowtail and monarch butterflies. If these butterflies don't visit your area, choose one of the other butterflies.

Outdoor Time

☼ Go on a walk and look for butterflies to observe. Allow the students to observe the butterflies and ask any questions they may have. You can use the information you have learned from reading the *Handbook of Nature Study* to answer their questions or to share information about what they are observing.

Coordinating Activities

✂ **Art** – (Butterfly Beauty) Have the students color and decorate with glitter and sequins a black-line or hand-drawn outline of a butterfly.

✂ **Snack** – (Like a Caterpillar) Let the students pretend to be caterpillars eating leaves. Use lettuce for the leaves.

✂ **Activity** – (Butterfly Symmetry) Using an eye dropper, have the students drop blobs of paint on one half of a piece of paper. Before the paint dries, have the students fold the paper in half and press so that the paint spreads out evenly on both sides. Then, cut out a half butterfly shape from the paper using the middle fold line as the middle of your butterfly. Open it up and let it dry. Talk about how a butterfly has symmetry (i.e., the design of its wings are the same on both sides) like the butterfly they made.

Write – Simple Notebooking

Student Diary

- ☐ **Main Idea Page** – Have the students color the coloring page found on SD p. 151.
- ☐ **Demonstration Sheet** – After you do the demonstration, fill out the demonstration sheet found on SD p. 152 with the students.
- ☐ **Nature Journal Sheet** – After you have your nature study time, fill out the nature journal sheet found on SD p. 153 with the students. The students can sketch what they have seen, or you can write down their observations.
- ☐ **Art Page** – Have the students use SD p. 154 to complete the art activity.

Lapbooking Templates

- 📁 **Weekly Mini-book** – Have the students cut out and color the Butterfly Mini-book on LT p. 62. You can have them cut out the main idea graphic included and glue it in the interior of the mini-book, or you can write a sentence with what they have learned from the week for them on the inside of the mini-book. Once the students are done, have them glue the booklet into the mini-lapbook.
- 📁 **Overall Lapbook** – Have the students add the page they painted to the "My Zoology Projects" pocket in the lapbook.

Week 5: Invertebrates

	2-Days-a-Week Schedule	
	Day 1	**Day 2**
Read	❑ Read the introduction with the students ❑ Read the selected pages in *The Usborne Children's Encyclopedia*	❑ Choose one or more of the additional books to read from this week
Do	❑ Complete the Scientific Demonstration "Attracting Ants" ❑ Eat "Edible Invertebrates" for snack	❑ Complete the Nature Study "Garden Snails" ❑ Do the "Worm Trails" activity
Write	❑ Color the main idea page ❑ Fill out the demonstration sheet	❑ Fill out the nature journal sheet ❑ Complete the art page

	5-Days-a-Week Schedule				
	Day 1	**Day 2**	**Day 3**	**Day 4**	**Day 5**
Read	❑ Read the introduction with the students	❑ Read the selected pages in *The Usborne Children's Encyclopedia*	❑ Choose one or more of the additional books to read from this week	❑ Choose one or more of the additional books to read from this week	
Do	❑ Eat "Edible Invertebrates" for snack	❑ Complete the Scientific Demonstration "Attracting Ants"	❑ Work on the activity "Styrofoam Spiders"	❑ Do the "Worm Trails" activity	❑ Complete the Nature Study "Garden Snails"
Write	❑ Color the main idea page	❑ Fill out the demonstration sheet	❑ Complete the Invertebrates Mini-book	❑ Complete the art page	❑ Fill out the nature journal sheet

Read – Information Gathering

Weekly Topic

✿ Invertebrates, like snails and worms, have no backbones.

Scripted Introduction

Have pictures of invertebrates out on the table in front of you. Say to the students:

> Humans are vertebrates because we have backbones. The human backbone is called the spine.

> **?** Can you find your spine?

Have the students feel the backs of their necks to find their spines. Then say:

> Good job! There are many animals that do have backbones like us, but there are also animals that do not have backbones. They are called invertebrates.

Pause to point out the pictures you have of invertebrates and name the animals before continuing:

> This week, we are going to look closer at insects, snails, and worms, which are animals that have no backbones. Insects, snails, and worms are all invertebrates.

Read–Alouds

Encyclopedia Pages

📖 *The Usborne Children's Encyclopedia* pp. 74-75 "Creepy Crawlies"

Library Books to Look For

📖 *No Backbone! the World of Invertebrates* by Natalie Lunis
📖 *I Wonder What It's Like to Be an Earthworm* by Erin M. Hovanec
📖 *Are You a Snail?* (Backyard Books) by Judy Allen

Do – Hands-on Projects

Scientific Demonstration: Attracting Ants

Materials Needed

✓ Plate
✓ Several types of food (i.e., bread, cheese, crackers, honey, and fruit)

Steps to Complete

1. Read the following introduction to your students:

   Remember earlier we talked about how insects are invertebrates? Ants are a type of insect, making them invertebrates. Today, we are going to attempt to attract these insects so we can observe them!

2. Have the students choose several different types of food, such as bread, cheese, crackers, honey, and fruit. Have them set a small amount of their selection in different sections on a plate.

3. Take the students outside, and find a place on the ground to set their plate where it can sit undisturbed for several hours.

4. Head back inside and wait 40 to 60 minutes before heading back outside to check on the plate.

5. Have the students observe the plate to see which insects visit it. Ask them:

   ? Did we get ants to visit our plate?

   ? What food did the ants go to first?

Explanation

Read the following explaination to the students:

We saw insects, like ants visiting our plate. The ants seem to be attracted the most to food that had sugar, such as honey and fruit. This is because ants prefer the food with the highest amount and most digestible source of energy, which is sugar!

Nature Study: Garden Snails

This week, you will look for garden snails in your backyard or park. Be sure to also point out any other invertebrates you run across, such as worms and insects.

Preparation

↻ Read pp. 416-418 in the *Handbook of Nature Study* to learn more about invertebrates and the garden snail.

Outdoor Time

✿ Go on a walk and look for snails and other invertebrates to observe. Allow the students to observe them and ask any questions they may have. You can use the information you have learned from reading the *Handbook of Nature Study* to answer their questions or to share information about what they are observing.

Coordinating Activities

✄ Art – (Worm Trails) Have the students drag a piece of thick string through paint. Then have them move the piece of string across a sheet of paper like a worm.

✄ Snack – (Edible Invertebrates) Serve the students escargot (snails). Just kidding! Tell the students that in other countries they do eat invertebrates, such as snails and crickets, but today we are going to eat worms. Then, serve them gummy worms!

✄ Activity – (Styrofoam Spider) Have the students make a spider out of black pipe cleaners and Styrofoam balls. You will need the following: one large and one small Styrofoam balls, black paint, googly eyes, and black pipe cleaners. Begin by painting one small and one large Styrofoam ball black. Once they are dry, add googly eyes to the smaller Styrofoam ball for the head and attach it to the larger ball using a small piece of pipe cleaner. Then, cut four pipe cleaners in half and attach them to either side of the large Styrofoam ball for the eight spider legs.

Write – Simple Notebooking

Student Diary

☐ Main Idea Page – Have the students color the coloring page found on SD p. 155.

☐ Demonstration Sheet – After you do the demonstration, fill out the demonstration sheet found on SD p. 156 with the students.

☐ Nature Journal Sheet – After you have your nature study time, fill out the nature journal sheet found on SD p. 157 with the students. The students can sketch what they have seen, or you can write down their observations.

☐ Art Page – Have the students use SD p. 158 to complete the art activity.

Lapbooking Templates

📁 Weekly Mini-book – Have the students cut out and color the Invertebrates Mini-book on LT p. 64. You can have them cut out the main idea graphic included and glue it in the interior of the mini-book, or you can write a sentence with what they have learned from the week for them on the inside of the mini-book. Once the students are done, have them glue the booklet into the mini-lapbook.

📁 Overall Lapbook – Have the students add the page they painted to the "My Zoology Projects" pocket in the lapbook.

Week 6: Fish

2-Days-a-Week Schedule		
	Day 1	**Day 2**
Read	❑ Read the introduction with the students ❑ Read the selected pages in *The Usborne Children's Encyclopedia*	❑ Choose one or more of the additional books to read from this week
Do	❑ Go on a Field Trip ❑ Eat "Goldfish Crackers" for snack	❑ Complete the Nature Study "Fish" ❑ Do the "Sparkle Fish" activity
Write	❑ Color the main idea page ❑ Fill out the demonstration sheet when you get home	❑ Fill out the nature journal sheet ❑ Complete the art page

5-Days-a-Week Schedule					
	Day 1	**Day 2**	**Day 3**	**Day 4**	**Day 5**
Read	❑ Read the introduction with the students		❑ Read the selected pages in *The Usborne Children's Encyclopedia*	❑ Choose one or more of the additional books to read from this week	❑ Choose one or more of the additional books to read from this week
Do	❑ Eat "Goldfish Crackers" for snack	❑ Go on a Field Trip	❑ Work on the activity "Go Fishing"	❑ Do the "Sparkle Fish" activity	❑ Complete the Nature Study "Fish"
Write	❑ Color the main idea page	❑ Fill out the demonstration sheet when you get home	❑ Complete the Fish Mini-book	❑ Complete the art page	❑ Fill out the nature journal sheet

Read – Information Gathering

Weekly Topic

ϟ Fish have gills so they can breathe underwater.

Scripted Introduction

Have pictures of fish out on the table in front of you. Say to the students:

> During this unit, we are going to look at several different types of animals. This week, we are going to look at fish.
>
> **?** What do you know about fish?

Let the students answer, correcting any false information and agreeing with correct facts. Then say to the students:

> That's great!
>
> All fish have gills so that they can breathe underwater. Fish also have scales all over their bodies and they have fins instead of legs and arms to help them move through the water.
>
> Fish are cold-blooded, which means that they don't produce their own heat like we mammals do. This week, we are going to learn more about fish!

Read–Alouds

Encyclopedia Pages

📖 *The Usborne Children's Encyclopedia* pp. 80-81 "Underwater Life"

Library Books to Look For

📖 *What's It Like to Be a Fish?* (Let's-Read-and-Find Out Science 1) by Wendy Pfeffer and Holly Keller
📖 *Rainbow Fish Big Book* by Marcus Pfister Herbert and J. Alison James
📖 *Fish Eyes: A Book You Can Count On* by Lois Ehlert

Do – Hands-on Projects

Field Trip

1. Read the following introduction to your students:

> Remember earlier we saw pictures of fish? This week we are going to go on a field trip to see fish and the other animals we have learned about in this unit!

2. Go on a field trip to an aquarium or a zoo to observe fish and the other animals that you have learned about over this unit.

(Alternative Option)

If you do not live near an aquarium or zoo, you can set up your own goldfish tank for this week's hands-on science project. The following website has detailed instructions on how to set up a goldfish tank:

🖱 https://www.cuteness.com/article/set-up-goldfish-bowl

Once the tank is set up, have the students observe the goldfish's behavior.

Nature Study: Fish

This week, you will look at fish in your area.

Preparation

↻ Read pp. 144-169 in the *Handbook of Nature Study* to learn more about fish. If you're lucky enough to live near a brook or stream, you can read about all the fish in your area from the section. If not, concentrate on the goldfish section found on pp. 144-147.

Outdoor Time

☼ Go on a walk and look for a brook, stream, or pond with fish in it to observe. Allow the students to observe the fish and ask any questions they may have. You can use the information you have learned from reading the *Handbook of Nature Study* to answer their questions or to share information about what they are observing. If you cannot find fish to observe, use a goldfish for your nature study time.

Coordinating Activities

✂ **Art** – (Sparkle Fish) Give the students a black-line image or hand-drawn outline of a fish. Have them use watercolor paints to paint their own rainbow fish. Then, you can have them decorate it with glitter and other sparkly things.

✂ **Snack** – (Goldfish Crackers) Have some goldfish crackers for snack time this week.

✂ **Activity** – (Go Fishing) For this game, you will need construction paper, several paper clips, a magnet, a dowel rod, and string. Begin by cutting out five red, four blue, three green and two yellow fish. Attach a paper clip to the end of each of the fish, and place them all into a bucket or box that is not transparent. Next, tie a magnet to a string and tie the string to a pole, either a dowel rod or a cardboard tube. Then, go fishing and see what you catch. The red fish are worth one point each, the blue fish are worth two points each, the green fish are worth five points each, and the yellow fish are worth ten points each. The person with the most points wins the game.

Write – Simple Notebooking

Student Diary

- ☐ Main Idea Page – Have the students color the coloring page found on SD p. 159.

- ☐ Demonstration Sheet – After you do the demonstration, fill out the demonstration sheet found on SD p. 160 with the students.

- ☐ Nature Journal Sheet – After you have your nature study time, fill out the nature journal sheet found on SD p. 161 with the students. The students can sketch what they have seen, or you can write down their observations.

- ☐ Art Page – Have the students use SD p. 162 to complete the art activity.

Lapbooking Templates

- ☐ Weekly Mini-book – Have the students cut out and color the Fish Mini-book on LT p. 64. You can have them cut out the main idea graphic included and glue it in the interior of the mini-book, or you can write a sentence with what they have learned from the week for them on the inside of the mini-book. Once the students are done, have them glue the booklet into the mini-lapbook.

- ☐ Overall Lapbook – Have the students add the page they painted to the "My Zoology Projects" pocket in the lapbook.

Intro to Science
Appendix

Rock Candy Recipe

Ingredients

- ✓ Food coloring
- ✓ Glass jars
- ✓ Oven mitts
- ✓ Saucepan
- ✓ Spoons
- ✓ Pencils
- ✓ Paper
- ✓ Binder clips
- ✓ Cotton string
- ✓ 3 Cups Sugar

Steps to Make

1. Begin by boiling about one cup water and add about two cups of sugar.
2. Pour the water into a glass jar and then slowly stir in remaining sugar, about a teaspoon at a time. (*Note—Be careful to not rush this step.*)
3. Continue stirring until the sugar no longer dissolves and starts to collect at the bottom of the jar.
4. Choose a color for your crystals and add a couple of drops of food coloring.
5. Tie one end of a piece of string around the middle of a pencil and tie a paper clip to the other end.
6. Place the pencil over the jar so that the string hangs down and the paper clip almost touches the bottom of the jar.
7. Allow the jar to sit someplace where it will be undisturbed.
8. Check after about 24 to 48 hours, and you'll see colorful crystals forming on the paper clip.
9. Let the solution sit for several weeks and you will have some rock candy to eat!

The Water Cycle

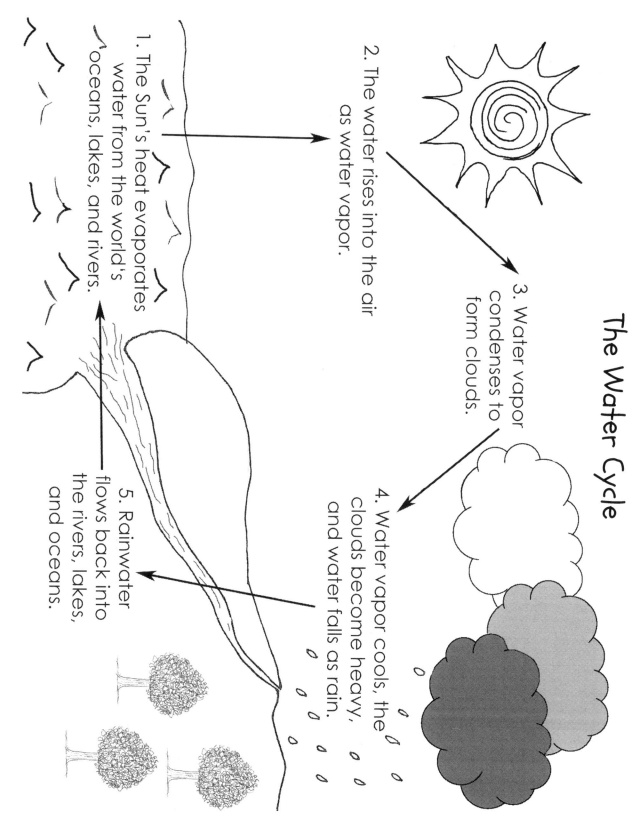

1. The Sun's heat evaporates water from the world's oceans, lakes, and rivers.

2. The water rises into the air as water vapor.

3. Water vapor condenses to form clouds.

4. Water vapor cools, the clouds become heavy, and water falls as rain.

5. Rainwater flows back into the rivers, lakes, and oceans.

Cloud Matching Templates

Weather Stickers

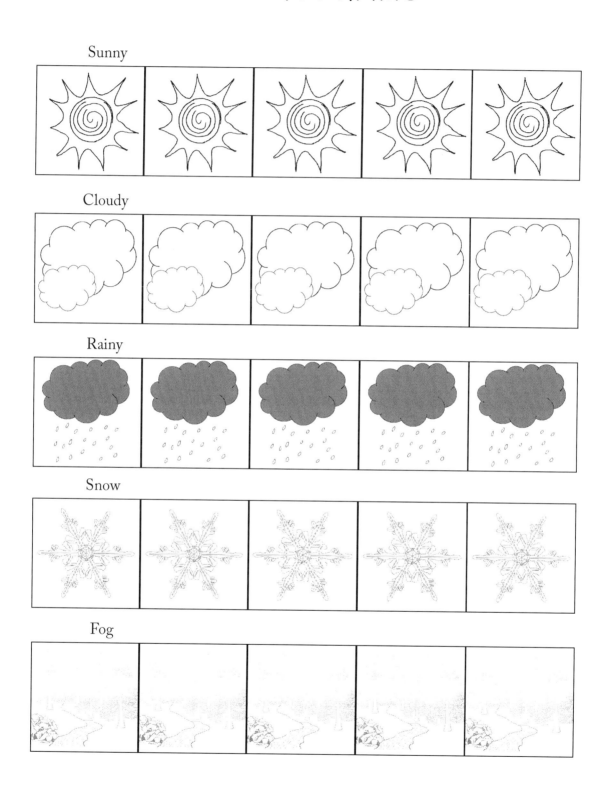

Parts of a Flower

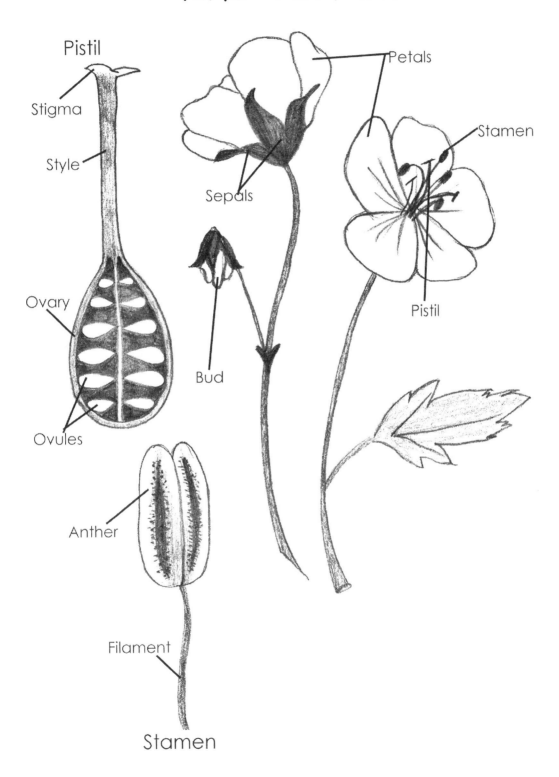

Pistil

Stigma

Style

Ovary

Ovules

Petals

Sepals

Stamen

Pistil

Bud

Anther

Filament

Stamen

Parts of a Seed

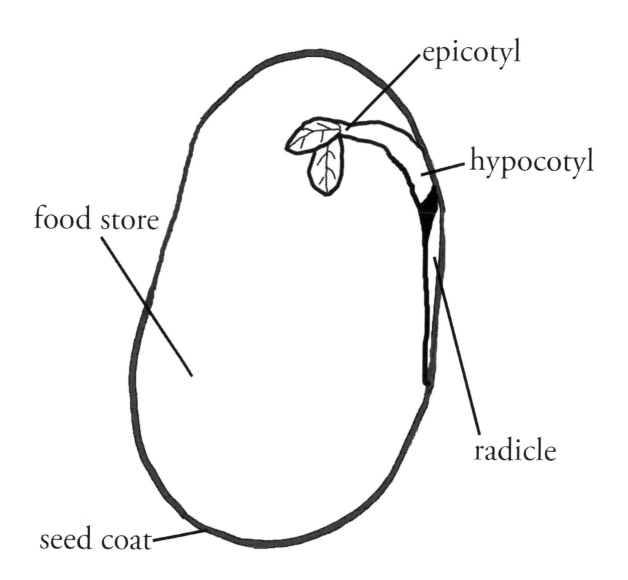

epicotyl

hypocotyl

food store

radicle

seed coat

Butterfly Life Cycle Pictures

Butterflies lay eggs on leaves.

Caterpillars hatch out of the eggs and eat the leaves.

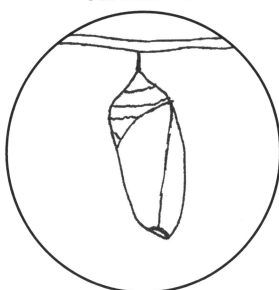

When they are full, caterpillars make a chrysalis.

A butterfly emerges from the chrysalis.

Intro to Science

General Templates

Narration Sheet

Project Record Sheet

Paste a picture of your

project in this box.

What I Learned:

_____

_____

_____

_____

_____

_____

_____

202

Two Days a Week Schedule

Day 1	Day 2
❏	❏
❏	❏
❏	❏
❏	❏
❏	❏
❏	❏

Things to Prepare

❏

❏

❏

Notes

Five Days a Week Schedule

Day 1	Day 2	Day 3	Day 4	Day 5
❑	❑	❑	❑	❑
❑	❑	❑	❑	❑
❑	❑	❑	❑	❑
❑	❑	❑	❑	❑

All Week Long

❑

❑

Things to Prepare

❑

❑

❑

Notes

Intro to Science
Library Book List

Library Book List

Unit 1: Intro to Chemistry

Week 1
- *What is the world made of? All about solids, liquids and gases (Let's Read and Find out About Science)* by Kathleen Weidner Zoehfeld and Paul Meisel
- *Change It!: Solids, Liquids, Gases and You (Primary Physical Science)* by Adrienne Mason and Claudia Davila
- *Solids, Liquids and Gases (Starting with Science)* by Ray Boudreau

Week 2
- *Liquids* (States of Matter) by Carol Ryback and Jim Mezzanotte
- *Lulu's Lemonade* (Math Matters) by Barbara Derubertis and Paige Billin-Frye

Week 3
- *What Is Density?* (Rookie Read-About Science) by Joanne Barkan
- *Will It Float or Sink?* (Rookie Read-About Science) by Melissa Stewart

Week 4
- *Crystals (The Golden Science Close-up Series)* by Robert A. Bell
- *Rock and Minerals (Eye Wonder)* by DK Publishing

Week 5
- *All the Colors of the Rainbow* (Rookie Read-About Science) by Allan Fowler
- *The Magic School Bus Makes A Rainbow: A Book About Color* by Joanna Cole
- *I Love Colors!* (Hello Reader!, Level 1) by Hans Wilhelm

Week 6
- *Freezing and Melting* (First Step Nonfiction) by Robin Nelson
- *Solids, Liquids, And Gases* (Rookie Read-About Science) by Ginger Garrett

Unit 2: Intro to Physics

Week 1
- *Gravity Is a Mystery* (Let's-Read-and-Find... Science 2) by Franklyn M. Branley and Edward Miller
- *What Is Gravity?* (Rookie Read-About Science) by Lisa Trumbauer
- *Gravity* (Blastoff! Readers: First Science) by Kay Manolis
- *Galileo's Leaning Tower Experiment* (Junior Library Guild Selection) by Wendy Macdonald and Paolo Rui

Week 2

- *Magnets* (All Aboard Science Reader) by Anne Schreiber and Adrian C. Sinnott
- *What Makes a Magnet?* (Let's-Read-and-Find... Science 2) by Franklyn M. Branley and True Kelley
- *Magnets: Pulling Together, Pushing Apart* (Amazing Science) by Natalie M. Boyd

Week 3

- *Inclined Planes to the Rescue* (First Facts) by Thales and Sharon
- *Inclined Planes and Wedges* (Early Bird Physics Series) by Sally M. Walker
- *What are Inclined Planes?* (Looking at Simple Machines) by Helen Frost

Week 4

- *The Magic School Bus and the Electric Field Trip* by Joanna Cole

Week 5

- *Pull, Lift, and Lower: A Book About Pulleys* (Amazing Science: Simple Machines) by Dahl
- *What Is a Pulley?* (Welcome Books) by Lloyd G. Douglas

Week 6

- *All About Light* (Rookie Read-About Science) by Lisa Trumbauer
- *Exploring Light* (How Does Science Work?) by Carol Ballard
- *The Magic School Bus: Gets A Bright Idea, The: A Book About Light* by Nancy White

Unit 3: Intro to Geology

Week 1

- *Mary Anning: Fossil Hunter* by Sally M. Walker and Phyllis V. Saroff
- *Viewfinder: Fossils* by Douglas Palmer and Neil D. L. Clark
- *What Do You Know About Fossils?* (20 Questions: Science) by Suzanne Slade
- *Fossils Tell of Long Ago* (Let's-Read-and-Find Out Science 2) by Aliki

Week 2

- *Looking at Rocks* (My First Field Guides) by Jennifer Dussling and Tim Haggerty
- *Rocks: Hard, Soft, Smooth, and Rough* (Amazing Science) by Rosinsky, Natalie M, John, and Matthew
- *Rocks and Fossils* (Science Kids) by Chris Pellant
- *Rocks! Rocks! Rocks!* by Nancy Elizabeth Wallace

Week 3

- *Metamorphic Rocks* (Earth Rocks!) by Holly Cefrey
- *I Love Rocks* (Rookie Readers, Level B) by Cari Meister and Terry Sirrell

Week 4

- 📖 *National Geographic Readers: Volcanoes!* by Anne Schreiber
- 📖 *Jump into Science: Volcano!* by Ellen J. Prager and Nancy Woodman
- 📖 *Volcanoes* (Let's-Read-and-Find... Science 2) by Franklyn M. Branley and Megan Lloyd
- 📖 *The Magic School Bus Blows Its Top: A Book About Volcanoes* (Magic School Bus) by Gail Herman and Bob Ostrom

Week 5

- 📖 *Sedimentary Rocks* (Earth Rocks!) by Holly Cefrey
- 📖 *Earthsteps: A Rock's Journey through Time* by Diane Nelson Spickert and Marianne D. Wallace

Week 6

- 📖 *You Can Use a Compass* (Rookie Read-About Science) by Lisa Trumbauer
- 📖 *North, South, East, and West* (Rookie Read-About Science) by Allan Fowler
- 📖 *Maps and Globes* by Jack Knowlton and Harriet Barton

Unit 4: Intro to Meteorlogy

Week 1

- 📖 *The Sun: Our Nearest Star* (Let's-Read-and-Find Out) by Franklyn M. Branley and Edward Miller
- 📖 *Wake Up, Sun!* (Step-Into-Reading, Step 1) by David L. Harrison
- 📖 *The Sun Is My Favorite Star* by Frank Asch

Week 2

- 📖 *The Water Cycle* (First Facts, Water All Around) by Rebecca Olien
- 📖 *The Magic School Bus Wet All Over: A Book About The Water Cycle* by Pat Relf and Carolyn Bracken

Week 3

- 📖 *Watching the Seasons* (Welcome Books) by Edana Eckart
- 📖 *Sunshine Makes the Seasons* (Let's-Read-and-Find... Science 2) by Franklyn M. Branley and Michael Rex
- 📖 *Our Seasons* by Ranida T. Mckneally and Grace Lin

Week 4

- 📖 *Feel the Wind* (Let's-Read-and-Find... Science 2) by Arthur Dorros
- 📖 *The Wind Blew* by Pat Hutchins
- 📖 *Can You See the Wind?* (Rookie Read-About Science) by Allan Fowler

Week 5

- *Tornado Alert* (Let's-Read-and-Find... Science 2) by Franklyn M. Branley and Giulio Maestro
- *Tornados!* (DK READERS) by DK Publishing
- *The Terrifying Tub Tornado* by Ann K. Larson

Week 6

- *What Is a Thermometer* (Rookie Read-About Science) by Lisa Trumbauer
- *Thermometers* (First Facts. Science Tools) by Adele Richardson
- *Temperature* (Blastoff! Readers, First Science) by Kay Manolis
- *Too, Too Hot* (Reader's Clubhouse Level 1 Reader) by Judy Kentor Schmauss

Unit 5: Intro to Botany

Week 1

- *From Seed to Plant* (Rookie Read-About Science) by Allan Fowler
- *From Seed to Plant* by Gail Gibbons

Week 2

- *The Reason for a Flower* (Ruth Heller's World of Nature) by Ruth Heller
- *Planting a Rainbow* by Lois Ehler

Week 3

- *The Magic School Bus Plants Seeds: A Book About How Living Things Grow* by Joanna Cole
- *Seeds* by Ken Robbins
- *A Fruit Is a Suitcase for Seeds* by Jean Richards and Anca Hariton
- *Curious George Plants a Seed* (Curious George Early Readers) by H. A. Rey

Week 4

- *Leaves* (Plant Parts series) by Vijaya Bodach,
- *I Am A Leaf* (Level 1 - Hello Reader) by Jean Marzollo and Judith Moffatt
- *Leaves* by David Ezra Stein

Week 5

- *Stems* (Plant Parts) by Vijaya Bodach
- *Plant Stems & Roots* (Look Once, Look Again Science Series) by David M. Schwartz
- *Stems* (First Step Nonfiction) by Melanie Mitchell

Week 6

- *Roots* (First Step Nonfiction) by Melanie Mitchell
- *Roots* (Plant Parts series) by Vijaya Bodach

📖 *Plant Plumbing: A Book About Roots and Stems* (Growing Things) by Susan Blackaby and Charlene Delage

Unit 6: Intro to Zoology

Week 1

📖 *About Mammals: A Guide For Children* by Cathryn Sill and John Sill

📖 *Eye Wonder: Mammals* (Eye Wonder) by Sarah Walker

📖 *Is a Camel a Mammal?* by Tish Rabe and Jim Durk

📖 *Animals Called Mammals* (What Kind of Animal Is It?) by Bobbie Kalman

Week 2

📖 *Miles and Miles of Reptiles: All About Reptiles* by Tish Rabe and Aristides Ruiz

📖 *Eye Wonder: Reptiles* (Eye Wonder) by Simon Holland

📖 *Reptiles* (True Books : Animals) by Melissa Stewart

📖 *Fun Facts About Snakes!* (I Like Reptiles and Amphibians!) by Carmen Bredeson

Week 3

📖 *About Birds: A Guide for Children* by Cathryn Sill and John Sill

📖 *Fine Feathered Friends: All About Birds* by Tish Rabe

📖 *How Do Birds Find Their Way?* (Let's-Read-and-Find Out Science 2) by Roma Gans

📖 *The Magic School Bus Flies from the Nest* by Joanna Cole and Carolyn Bracken

Week 4

📖 *Butterfly House* by Eve Bunting and Greg Shed

📖 *A Butterfly Grows* (Green Light Readers Level 2) by Stephen R. Swinburne

📖 *From Caterpillar to Butterfly: Following the Life Cycle* by Suzanne Slade

📖 *The Life of a Butterfly* by Clare Hibbert

Week 5

📖 *No Backbone! the World of Invertebrates* by Natalie Lunis

📖 *I Wonder What It's Like to Be an Earthworm* by Erin M. Hovanec

📖 *Are You a Snail?* (Backyard Books) by Judy Allen

Week 6

📖 *What's It Like to Be a Fish?* (Let's-Read-and-Find Out Science 1) by Wendy Pfeffer

📖 *Rainbow Fish Big Book* by Marcus Pfister Herbert and J. Alison James

📖 *Fish Eyes: A Book You Can Count On* by Lois Ehlert

Made in the USA
Middletown, DE
17 August 2024